TOPICS IN THE ANALYSIS OF CAUSATIVES

WITH AN ACCOUNT OF HINDI PARADIGMS

Topics in the Analysis of Causatives

with
an Account of Hindi Paradigms

by Anuradha Saksena

UNIVERSITY OF CALIFORNIA PRESS
Berkeley   Los Angeles   London

UNIVERSITY OF CALIFORNIA PUBLICATIONS IN LINGUISTICS

Editorial Board: William Bright, Wallace Chafe, Paul Kay,
Ronald Langacker, Margaret Langdon, Paul Schachter

Volume 98

Issue Date: August 1982

UNIVERSITY OF CALIFORNIA PRESS
BERKELEY AND LOS ANGELES, CALIFORNIA

UNIVERSITY OF CALIFORNIA PRESS, LTD.
LONDON, ENGLAND

O ✓

ISBN: 0-520-09659-2
LIBRARY OF CONGRESS CATALOG NUMBER: 82-60090

Library of Congress Cataloging in Publication Data

Saksena, Anuradha.
  Topics in the analysis of causatives.

  (University of California publications in linguistics;
v. 98)
  Includes bibliographical references.
  1. Causative (Linguistics) 2. Hindi language—
Causative. I. Title. II. Series.
P292.S24 1982   415   82-60090
ISBN 0-520-09659-2

Contents

Acknowledgments

This monograph is a revised and extended version of my UCLA doctoral dissertation. As such, it would not have been possible without the support of my doctoral committee: Paul Schachter (chairman), William Bright, Victoria Fromkin, Earl Rand, and Stanley Wolpert.

Professors Schachter and Bright read several drafts of this material, and it has profited greatly from their critical reading and many substantive suggestions, and from their respective interests in nontransformational grammars and in Hindi linguistics.

This work has also benefited from the comments of Professor Bruce Pray of the University of California at Berkeley and Professor Colin Masica of the University of Chicago, who served as expert readers for the University of California Press. The specific, detailed comments of Professor Masica have been particularly helpful.

Material from this monograph has been presented at various meetings and in journals, eliciting comments and suggestions from many linguists. This feedback has proved most valuable.

A modified version of Chapter II is scheduled to appear in Journal of Linguistics, and this material is presented here with copyright permission from the Cambridge University Press, Cambridge, England.

A modified version of Chapter III appeared as "The Source of Causative Contrast" in Lingua 51:125-136, and this chapter is presented here with copyright permission from North-Holland Publishing Company, Amsterdam.

The material of Chapters IV and V first appeared as "The Affected Agent" in Language 56.4:812-826 and is presented here with copyright permission from the Linguistic Society of America, Washington, D.C.

A modified version of Chapter VI is scheduled to appear in Language 58.4, and this material is also presented here with copyright permission from the Linguistic Society of America, Washington, D.C.

Material from Chapters VIII and IX first appeared as "Causative Relations in Hindi" in General Linguistics 20.1:23-28, and is presented here with copyright permission from The Pennsylvania State University Press, Pennsylvania.

Abstract

Hindi is a particularly useful language for the study
of causatives, since it yields paradigms with
morphologically explicit four-way contrasts. Much work on
these causatives has already been undertaken, including
applications of the Case Grammar (Balachandran 1973) and
transformational, Generative Semantics (Kachru 1966, 1971;
Kleiman 1971) models. However, these earlier studies have
failed to notice many generalizations that are crucial to
the analysis of causatives.

For example, Hindi data provide many counterexamples
to some basic assumptions of Case Grammar and/or Generative
Semantics: that transitives are derived from intransitives
(Chapter II); that causative contrast is an extra agent
contrast (Chapter III); that causee case marking correlates
with transitivity, or with case categories (Chapter IV);
that case categories are mutually distinct semantic
primitives (Chapter V); that the distinction between
contactive and noncontactive causation is a 'stage' of
causation and one that involves an intermediary (Chapter
VI); and that causative generalizations are
transformationally productive (Chapter VIII).

Rather, the data point to a new set of
generalizations: an intransitive rule (Chapter II);

causativization as a topicalization mechanism (Chapter III);
the contrasts of affected vs. nonaffected agents (Chapters
IV and V), involved vs. noninvolved causers, and contactive
vs. noncontactive causation (Chapter VI); a set of abstract
semantic   parameters   (Chapter   VII), and a lexicalist
framework (Chapters VIII and IX).

Abbreviations/Glossary

A(gt)   Agent

Base   Basic verb, not derived from any other

CG   Case Grammar

c.m.   case marking(s)

DC   Base verb plus the suffix -aa

GS   Generative Semantics

IC   Base verb plus the suffix -vaa

Intr   short-stem-vowel intransitive verb derived
            from Tr

O(bj)   Object

s.o.   someone

stg   something

T   transformation(al)

Tr   long-stem-vowel transitive verb, a   subset
            of Base

1

INTRODUCTION

Hindi is a particularly valuable language for the discussion of causatives, for in few languages is the phenomenon so well entrenched. First, it applies to the overwhelming majority of verbs; second, it is morphologically overt; and third, it presents up to a four-way contrast. Thus, the data are rich in easily accessible evidence.

This study of Hindi causatives has two goals. First, it provides a systematization of the Hindi data; second, it brings the generalizations discovered to bear on key issues in the description of causatives.

1. PREVIEW

This work will justify the following strictly morphologically based classification of Hindi paradigms.

1.1 Three-Member Paradigms

Base verbs (transitive or intransitive, and of any morphological shape) can potentially take a suffix -aa (termed DC), and a suffix -vaa (termed IC), as shown in (1).

(1) Base   DC   IC

     paṛh   paṛh-aa   paṛh-vaa
     study   teach   have (s.o.) study

     ban   ban-aa   ban-vaa
     get made   make   have (stg) made

     caṛh   caṛh-aa   caṛh-vaa
     climb   make (s.o.) climb   have (s.o.) climb

     hãs   hãs-aa   hãs-vaa
     laugh   make (s.o.) laugh   have (s.o.) laugh

     kar   kar-aa   kar-vaa
     do   have (s.o.) do   have (s.o.) do

These morphological shapes are modified by regular morpho-phonological rules such as schwa-deletion (e.g., /badal/-/badl-aa/ 'change') and stem vowel shortening before a long vowel suffix (as in /maan/-/man-aa/ 'agree'), but there are also many idiosyncrasies (Chapter VIII).

The DC suffix signifies that the verb is a causative with a personally involved causer, and the IC suffix signifies that the verb is a causative with a noninvolved causer.

The semantics of causer involvement (signified by -aa vs. -vaa) combines with a certain semantic property of verbs to yield an additional semantic contrast. If the subject of the Base verb is +affected (= marked by the c.m. -<u>koo</u> or <u>0</u>

in the corresponding causative), then -<u>aa</u> suffixation

results in direct, contactive causation; if however, the

subject of the Base verb is -affected (= marked by the c.m.

-<u>see</u> in the corresponding causative), -<u>aa</u> suffixation

results in indirect, noncontactive causation. The IC -<u>vaa</u>

suffix, on the other hand, with all verbs uniformly yields

indirect, noncontactive causation.

   This means that if Base verbs have +affected subjects,

the DC and IC forms are contrastive with respect to

contactive vs. noncontactive causation, e.g., /paṛh-aa/

'teach' vs. /paṛh-vaa/ 'have study'; but if Base verbs have

-affected subjects, these forms alike signal noncontactive

causation, e.g., /kar-aa/, /kar-vaa/ 'have do'.

1.2 Four-Member Paradigms

   The basic three-way paradigm can be augmented by

another morphological contrast. If the Base verb has

transitive syntax <u>and</u> a long stem vowel (termed Tr), then we

can derive corresponding intransitives with a short stem

vowel (termed Intr), as shown in (2).

(2) <u>Intr</u>   <u>Tr</u>   <u>DC</u>   <u>IC</u>

     dikh   deekh   dikh-aa   dikh-vaa
     get seen   see   show   have (s.o.) show

     luṭ   luuṭ   luṭ-aa   luṭ-vaa
     get robbed   rob   squander   have plundered

     lad   laad   lad-aa   lad-vaa

get loaded   load   have loaded   have loaded

kaṭ   kaaṭ   kaṭ-aa   kaṭ-vaa
get cut   cut   have cut   have cut

/i/ in the Intr represents the -long counterpart of both /ee/ and /ii/, and /u/ the -long counterpart of both /oo/ and /uu/.

Earlier grammars, including transformational ones (Kachru 1966, Kleiman 1971), subordinate the morphological generalizations presented here in favor of a more abstract semantic classification of 'First' and 'Second' (semantic) stages of causativization.

2. TERMS

The previous section introduced four terms--Intr, Tr, DC, and IC--referring to the morphological derivation. Notice that the terms Intr and Tr are not synonymous with the terms _intransitive_ and _transitive_. For example, since Tr are defined as having a long stem vowel in addition to transitive syntax, this term cannot be applied to transitives which do not have a long stem vowel, e.g., the verb /paṛh/ 'read, study', or /ban-aa/ 'make', in the Base and DC columns, respectively, of (1). Similarly, since Intr are defined as being derived from Tr, the term Intr cannot be applied to short-stem-vowel intransitives if they do not have corresponding long-stem-vowel transitives, e.g., the verb /ban/ 'make' in the Base column of (1), which does not have a corresponding */baan/ 'make, Tr'.

Although DC and IC are the only morphological causatives, semantically, the term causative is equally appropriate for Tr, which are (semantically) in a causative relation to Intr. This means that (semantically) the term (non)causative is a relative notion--since the Tr are causatives compared to Intr, but noncausatives compared to DC and IC. Morphological claims will be based on a morphological definition, semantic claims on a semantic definition (of the term causative). This study is restricted to single-word causatives only, and does not include structures that involve overt embedding; moreover, the discussion avoids hypothetical verbs, and refers only to actual verbs and actual contrasts.

The term causer refers to the subject of a causative sentence, the term causee to that NP in causatives which is semantically equivalent to the subject of the noncausative. The term causative paradigm refers to the entire paradigm, including the noncausative.

The Case Grammar notions of a case frame as well as terms such as agent, patient (used synonymously with object), and instrument are used informally as convenient notions for discussing verb semantics; such use does not, however, connote acceptance of them as significant grammatical categories.

The terms lexical and productive are used in the normal linguistic sense without implying the specialized usage and claims (e.g., concerning simplex vs. complex) assigned to them in Shibatani (1975); the appendix shows this specialized usage to be neither necessary nor desirable.

3. GLOSSES

The Intr verbs find their closest English parallel in pseudo-intransitives such as 'The book reads easily'. Since English lacks this usage for most Intr verbs, I have had to use the words 'be' and 'get' in the glosses. This practice distorts the meaning analogously to rendering 'The book reads easily' as 'The book gets/was read easily'.

The glosses 'make' and 'have' are used contrastively, with the former signifying direct, contactive causation, the latter indirect, noncontactive causation.

An IC sentence can be glossed as being the noncontactive causative of either the Intr, the Tr, or the DC verb. For example, the IC /dikh-vaa/ can be glossed as either 'have (something) be seen', 'have (someone) see (something)', or 'have (someone) show (something)'; moreover, either the active or the passive version of these glosses are equally appropriate. To avoid being cumbersome,

only one of these glosses will be given at any one time,
with the understanding that the other readings are always
available.   Again, for the sake of conciseness, the NP's
'someone' and 'something' may be omitted when glossing
causative verbs.

        There are three morphologically overt case markers
that we need to be concerned with.   The c.m. -nee marks the
subject agent in the past and is glossed 'agt'.   The c.m.
-see marks a variety of roles, including the instrumental
and various nonsubject agents, and is glossed 'instr'.   The
c.m. -koo, which marks datives, experiencers, some causee
agents, and some patients, is glossed 'D/A'.   These glosses
serve   identification   purposes only, and do not make
substantive claims.

4. DATA

        The dialect reported here is my own,[1] and no claims
are made concerning either the normative value, or the
prevalence of the reported forms.

        Previous   readers have raised methodological questions
concerning this source of data.   For   example, Bruce Pray
(pers. comm.) feels that one ought not to generalize on the
basis of a single idiolect, and Colin Masica (pers. comm.)
notes that linguists do not make impartial informants for
their own work.[2] Elsewhere in the literature (Jain 1977),

the authenticity of certain idiolects has been questioned, and prescriptive norms are often felt important (cf. fn. 2) in Hindi linguistics. The author feels no obligation to resolve quarrels of this nature because the goal here is not to study variation, or set up prescriptive norms, but to provide a grammar open to empirical falsification.

This means that discussion of dialectal and idiolectal variation becomes meaningful only if it provides evidence for or against a proposed analysis. However, many instances of variation that are pointed out to me are irrelevant for this purpose. For example, I use the form /kar-aa/ 'do-past' [Chapter IV, example (14)] as an optional variant of /ki-yaa/, a usage that some (C. Masica, pers. comm.) find unauthentic. Use of either form has no bearing whatsoever on any of the proposals; thus, however interesting such data might be for a different type of work (e.g., one studying dialect differences, language change, the effect of other languages on Hindi, rule-generalization, etc.), it is without interest here.

As a further corollary, variant forms become an issue only if they involve counterevidence--examples which either destroy the support for a proposed analysis, or which suggest an alternate, better-motivated analysis. Again, the instances of variation that have been brought to my attention fail to serve this purpose. For example, in

Chapter II, some speakers (C. Masica, pers. comm.) may not
accept the forms ?/khai/ 'get eaten' and ?/kharid/ 'get
bought';[3] however, even if we were to discount these forms,
we would still be left with the many other arguments for the
proposed intransitive rule. In Chapter IV, some dialects
(Kachru 1971:79) do not yield sentences such as (33), though
others do (Balachandran 1973:50). Again, removal of these
sentences fails to detract from the proposed significance of
the affected agent. Finally, in Chapter VIII disagreement
with any individual example leaves a sufficient number of
problem-free examples so that the case for idiosyncrasy is
not influenced. In other words, minor variation does not
affect the proposed grammar; rather, such variation is
completely expected based on what we know about language
variation: that dialects and idiolects differ in peripheral
areas while sharing the major core.

To conclude, given the goals of this monograph,
criticism involving data becomes interesting and
resolveable if philosophical objections make way for
empirical argumentation.

NOTES

[1]I grew up in a middle-class, above average educated, 'joint family' in Lakhimpur-Kheri and Kanpur in the province of Uttar Pradesh. Many women in my extended family had advanced degrees in Hindi language and literature, and literary and linguistic discussions frequently took place at home. The children were sent to English-medium schools, but use of English at home or in written correspondence with friends and family was, and remains, prohibited.

[2]This remark was made with reference to my use of agentive passives that do not contain a negative, question word, conditional, etc. [as in Chapter III, sentence (44)]. This criticism is inappropriate for three reasons. First, though not the prescriptive norm, these sentences are amply documented in the literature (Kachru 1966:181-184, McGregor 1972:116). Second, I have not attached any significance (here or elsewhere) to the absence of the negative, etc. in my dialect; as such, these elements may be freely inserted without altering the argumentation. Third, my own proposal for the passive (Saksena 1978) argues against a transformational description. That analysis is helped, not hindered, by the prescriptively correct dialect for which the use of negatives, etc., with agentive passives is

mandatory, because these constitute further restrictions on
a passive transformation.

In short, my argument does not gain from the reporting
of affirmative agentive passives.

[3]Informants such as Said Ali of the Department of
Linguistics, UCLA, agree that these forms are used quite
commonly.

2

THE BASICNESS OF TRANSITIVES*

This chapter establishes Tr to be basic, and Intr derived, thus arguing against the traditional (Kellogg 1972) and transformational (Kachru 1966, 1971; Kleiman 1971) view that Tr are derived as causatives from Intr.

1. HYPOTHESIS

In the normal human world (unlike, say, a physics laboratory), events typically consist of agents affecting objects. As such, we expect that typically, objects will be conceptualized with an agent, leading to a transitive frame (AO_), rather than without an agent, in an intransitive frame (O_). It is true that intransitives of the type (A_), as well as of the type (O_) representing natural events would not pose conceptual difficulty; however, such verbs would be numerically limited. The hypothesis that the intransitive frame (O_), representing agent-motivated activity is conceptually difficult can be verified through several corollaries.

First,   (O_)   verbs   representing   agent-motivated

activity   are   comparatively   infrequent--i.e.,   limited   in

number or absent altogether in languages of the world.   For

example,   the   familiar   English   has only a handful of such

verbs as 'These shirts wash easily'.

Second, (O_) verbs representing agent-motivated events

are marked.   This claim can be verified with   minimal   pairs

from   English   where   we   can   compare   'The   window broke',

representing   a   natural   event,   to   'These   potatoes   bake

easily',   representing an agent-motivated event.   Unlike the

former, the latter is   marked--not   only   semantically,   but

also syntactically, since it requires an obligatory adverb.

Thus,   third,   in languages   like   Hindi   which   contain

sets   of   (AO_)   vs.   (O_)   verbs representing agent-motivated

activity, we expect that   the   former   will   be   basic,   the

latter derived.   The following chapter provides a validation

of this expectation.

2. THE DATA

Recall from Chapter   I   that   one   type   of   causative

paradigm has three members--Base, DC, and IC--illustrated in

(1).

(1) Base   DC   IC

    parh   parh-aa   parh-vaa
    study   teach   have (s.o.) study

caṛh	caṛh-aa	caṛh-vaa
climb	make (s.o.) climb	have (s.o.) climb
hãs	hãs-aa	hãs-vaa
laugh	make (s.o.) laugh	have (s.o.) laugh
kar	kar-aa	kar-vaa
do	have (s.o.) do	have (s.o.) do

The intransitives in the Base column of (1) are clearly basic. On rare occasion, these Base intransitives may have the form (O_) and represent agent-motivated activity; however, almost all of these verbs also have an (A__) reading which is the more basic.[1]

The second type of causative paradigm has four members, as illustrated in (2).

(2)

Intr	Tr	DC	IC
dikh	deekh	dikh-aa	dikh-vaa
get seen	see	show	have (s.o.) show
luṭ	luuṭ	luṭ-aa	luṭ-vaa
get robbed	rob	give away	have (s.o.) give away
lad	laad	lad-aa	lad-vaa
get loaded	load	have loaded	have loaded
kaṭ	kaaṭ	kaṭ-aa	kaṭ-vaa
get cut	cut	have cut	have cut

In the paradigms of (2), it is not immediately apparent whether the Intr or the Tr forms are basic.

3. EARLIER ANALYSES

Almost all Hindi grammars, both traditional (e.g.,
Kellogg 1972:252-257) and modern (e.g., Kachru 1966; 1971;
Kleiman 1971; Balachandran 1973:18-19), consider Intr verbs
to be basic, and Tr to be their First causatives; however, a
small minority has argued, not very convincingly, for an Tr
⟶ Intr derivation.

For example, Masica (1976:52) and Sharma (1972:116)
argue that the transitive is, in general, semantically more
basic than the pseudo-passive meaning (comparable to the
English 'These shirts iron well') of Intr. This argument is
well taken; however, by itself it is insufficient. In many
paradigms, the transitive semantics is expressed by the DC
form, e.g., /ban/ '(get) made' vs. /ban-aa/ 'make'. In such
pairs, it is doubtful that Sharma and Masica would wish to
regard the -aa-suffixed transitive as basic on semantic
grounds alone.

Additionally, Masica (1976:60) points out that if we
regard short-vowel Intr as basic, then we will have to
lengthen this vowel for (Tr) transitives and then reshorten
it for the DC and IC forms. If, however, we regard Tr as
basic, then a single rule of stem vowel shortening will
account for the short vowel of the Intr as well as the DC
and IC forms.

This argument fails because vowel shortening in the

semanto-syntactically diverse Intr, DC, and IC hardly constitute a single morpho-phonological rule. Furthermore, we need not worry about the reshortening of the stem vowel for the DC and IC forms because this task is accomplished by the general morphological rule that shortens stem vowels before long vowel suffixes. The same rule is needed for the shortening of stem vowels before the nominalizing suffix -aaii: thus, /saaf/ 'clean, adj', but /saf-aaii/ 'cleanliness'; /liip/ 'paint, vb', but /lip-aaii/ 'painting, n'; /luuṭ/ 'plunder, vb', but /luṭ-aaii/ 'plundering, n'. Similar stem vowel shortening occurs before the plural suffixes -ẽẽ, -õõ, and -ỹãã. Thus, we get /bahuu/ 'bride', but /bahu-ẽẽ, bahu-õõ/; /larkii/ 'girl', but /larki-ãã, larki-õõ/.

It is clear, then, that we need a stronger case for the basicness of Tr and the accompanying rule of intransitivization.

4. NEW ARGUMENTS

First, if Intr are regarded as basic, then we lose the morphological generalizations on the data. For example, we then need to recognize two kinds of paradigms, corresponding to (1) and (2). Morphologically (2) has three 'stages' of causativization, whereas (1) has only two; (2) introduces the first 'stage' of causativization by vowel lengthening,

(1) by -aa suffixation; (2) may introduce the second 'stage'
of causativization by -aa suffixation, (1) only by -vaa
suffixation.   In other words, with Intr as basic, we cannot
make any morphological generalizations. With Tr   as   basic,
on   the   other   hand,   we   can   make   the   significant
generalization that all Base verbs may causativize with a
suffix -aa and a suffix -vaa.

Second, causativization by -aa   and   -vaa   suffixation
does   not   need to refer to syntactic properties   such as the
case frame of the verb. However, causativization via vowel
lengthening   must   be syntactically restricted.   Though both
intransitives and transitives can   undergo   causativization,
only intransitives would do so via vowel lengthening.   Short
vowel transitives such as /paṛh/ 'study' never undergo vowel
lengthening to yield */paaṛh/ 'teach'.

Third, notice that short vowel intransitive verbs form
four-member paradigms [e.g., the paradigm for dikh in (2)]
as well as three-member paradigms [e.g.,   the   paradigm for
ban   in (1)]. This means that the transitivization approach
will be forced to mark all short   vowel   intransitives   with
diacritic features to classify them   either as Intr (and
causativizing via vowel lengthening) or as Base   (and
causativizing via -aa suffixation).

Fourth, vowel lengthening   in   transitivization would
not   be   phonologically   unique.   When short vowels in Intr

alternate with long vowels in Tr, one cannot predict whether /i/ and /u/ in the former will alternate in the latter with /ii/ and /uu/, or with /ee/ and /oo/. Thus, the Intr ⟶ Tr rule involves marking a large number of Intr verbs with an arbitrary feature to trigger a lowering of the lengthened vowels /ii/ and /uu/ to /ee/ and /oo/. With transitives as basic, however, the converse vowel shortening rule feeds into a persistent raising rule. The fact that there are no short /e/ and /o/ in Hindi phonology[2] is expressed by the persistent rule (3):

(3)

$$
\begin{bmatrix} V \\ -low \\ -long \end{bmatrix} \text{----> } [\ +high\ ]
$$

Thus, the results of /ee/ and /oo/ shortening in intransitivization would be 'linked' to the segment structure rule (3), yielding /i/ and /u/, as desired. Furthermore, when /ee/ vs. /i/ and /oo/ vs. /u/ alternation is attested elsewhere in Hindi phonology, it is the /ee/ and /oo/ forms that are basic. For example, the same alternation takes place before the nominalizing suffix -aaii. Thus, /soo/ 'sleep' yields /sulaaii/; /seek/ 'warm' yields /sikaaii/.

Fifth, Intr ⟶ Tr is not a productive rule, but Tr ⟶ Intr is. Where there are gaps in the data, given a Tr verb a speaker can usually form a corresponding Intr, e.g.,

/khariid/ 'buy' vs. ?/kharid/ 'get bought'; /khaa/ 'eat' vs. ?/khay/ 'get eaten'. However, given an intransitive verb with a short stem vowel one can never freely form a corresponding Tr by vowel lengthening, e.g., /ban/ 'get made' but */baan/ 'make'; /miṭ/ 'get rubbed away' but */miiṭ/ 'rub away'.

Finally, the intransitive rule has been productive historically. Thus, talking about intransitivization, Masica (1976:52) says:

> This is also the historical truth in a sense: it is known that many such derivations have indeed occurred and are still occurring--for the process is a productive one. What has apparently happened is that an old Indo-European process of apophony, which <u>did</u> produce transitives (Eng. <u>rise/raise</u>) has been extended analogically in reverse. The whole system has reorganized itself on a new principle.

Masica then gives one example of a historical derivation: /nikal/ 'emerge' was derived from /nikaal/ 'take out'.

Thus, positing a rule of transitivization to account for the Intr-Tr contrast, as earlier grammarians had done, introduces a tremendous complication in the grammar. A rule of intransitivization is far simpler. This finding is in keeping with the hypothesis presented at the outset that intransitive (0_) verbs representing agent-motivated activity are marked, and the corresponding transitive (AO_) verbs are unmarked.

NOTES

*A modified version of this chapter was presented at the 1980 LSA Summer Meeting.

[1]Thus, for example, although the Base verb /uth/ 'rise' permits an (O_) reading, as in (i), it also permits an (A_) reading, as in (ii).

    (i) saaman uṭh ga-yaa

       luggage rise comp verb

       The luggage (got) picked up.

    (ii) raam uṭh (gay)-aa

       Ram rise-past

       Ram got up.

Moreover, the (O_) usage of (i) is marginal, since unlike (ii), (i) is awkward without the compound verb _gayaa_, as can be seen in (iii).

    (iii)?saamaan uṭh-aa

       luggage rise-past

       The luggage rose.

One rare, possible example of a Base (O_) verb signifying agent-motivated activity that does not have an (A_) reading is /baj/ 'strike (e.g., bell)'.

[2]Saksena (1970) shows /ee/ and /oo/ to be +long.

3

CHARACTERIZING CAUSATIVE CONTRAST*

1. CURRENT VIEW

It is commonly believed that causatives differ
syntactically from noncausatives in the presence of an extra
agent in their case frames; i.e., in causative sentences,
the action of the noncausative is performed by a causative
agent. This belief is found in major cross-linguistic
studies. For example, Comrie (1976a:261) states:

> In general, a given causative verb will be expected to
> have one more noun phrase argument than the
> corresponding noncausative verb, since in addition to
> the subject and objects, if any, of that verb, there
> will be a noun phrase expressing the person or thing
> that causes, brings about that action. (Italics mine)

In his areal, cross-linguistic study of causativization,

Masica (1976:56) points out:

> In terms of a scheme of verbal "valences" (the number
> of agent or patient entities implied by a verb) each
> derivational step adds one: if V_i is 1 or 2, V_j is 2 or
> 3, and V_e is 3 or 4 ...Semantically, therefore,
> causative derivatives are always more complex than the
> verbs they are derived from.

Naturally, the belief that causatives have an extra

21

(agent) noun phrase has been built into the formal models for the analysis of causatives. Thus, in Case Grammar, causative case frames are distinguished from noncausative case frames by the presence of an extra case category, Agent. For example, the noncausative <u>break</u> occurs in the frame (_O); the causative <u>break</u> in the frame (_AO). In Generative Semantics, this 'extra' agent translates as the NP which is the subject of an abstract verb CAUSE under which the corresponding noncausative is embedded. Thus, the noncausative <u>break</u> surfaces from the configuration [NP V], while its causative counterpart surfaces from the configuration [NP CAUSE [NP V]].

These theoretical views have been adopted for specific analyses of the Hindi data. For example, Kachru (1966, 1971) and Kleiman (1971) adopt the Generative Semantics approach; Balachandran (1973) adopts the Case Grammar position. This chapter shows that such a description of Hindi causatives is incorrect.

2. COUNTEREVIDENCE

2.1 Intransitive-Transitive Contrast

Intr-Tr sentence pairs such as (1) vs. (2) can be used to show that causativization involves an extra agent.

(1) peer kat-aa

tree cut,Intr-past

The tree (got) cut.

(2) raam-nee peer̥ kaaṭ-aa

Ram-agt tree cut,Tr-past

Ram cut the tree.

However, almost all Intr sentences can optionally take an agent in nonsubject position, marked by the instrumental case marking -see. As a result, Intr and Tr have the same number of arguments; like the action of the Tr sentences, that of the Intr is performed by an agent. Yet, the Intr preserve their characteristic morphology and continue to contrast semanto-syntactically with their corresponding Tr.

(3) (raam-see) peer̥ kaṭ-aa

Ram-instr tree cut,Intr-past,m

The tree got cut by Ram.

(4) raam-nee peer̥ kaaṭ-aa

Ram-agt tree cut,Tr-past,m

Ram cut the tree.

(5) raam (mãã-see) piṭ-aa

Ram mother-instr beat,Intr-past

Ram (got) beaten by Mother.

(6) mãã-nee raam-koo piiṭ-aa

Mother-agt Ram-D/A beat,Tr-past

Mother beat Ram.

(7) (raam-see) kamraa put-aa

Ram-agt room paint,Intr-past

The room (got) painted by Ram.

(8) raam-nee kamraa poot-aa

Ram-agt room paint,Tr-past

Ram painted the room.

Syntactically, the contrast between the Intr vs. Tr of (3)-(8) lies in subjectivization. The Intr subjectivizes the patient; the Tr subjectivizes the agent. Semantically, both the Intr (3) and the Tr (4), for example, express the same fact, viz., that Ram cut the tree. However, the Intr (3) is a statement about the tree being cut, whereas the Tr (4) is a statement about Ram cutting the tree. Thus, the Tr (4) but not the Intr (3) attributes initiative to Ram.[1]

The Intr-Tr pairs (3)-(8) thus show that minimally, causative contrast is realized as subject contrast, not as extra agent contrast.

2.2 Transitive-Causative Contrast

The transitive-causative pair (9)-(10) can be used to show that causatives have an extra agent (compared to the corresponding noncausative transitive).

(9) raam-nee paath parh-aa

Ram-agt lesson study-past

Ram studied the lesson.

(10) maastar-nee raam-koo paath parh-aa-yaa

teacher-agt Ram-D/A lesson study-DC-past

The teacher taught Ram the lesson.

However, many transitives can optionally take an agent that is semantically equivalent to the subject of the corresponding causative; this agent appears in nonsubject position, marked by the instrumental c.m. -<u>see</u>. Despite this optional agent, these transitives retain their morphological shape and continue to contrast semanto-syntactically with their corresponding causatives.

(11) raam-nee (maastar-see) paath parh-aa

      Ram-agt teacher-instr lesson study,Base-past

      *Ram studied the lesson from the teacher.

      Ram was taught the lesson by the teacher.

(12) maastar-nee raam-koo paath parh-aa-yaa

      teacher-agt Ram-D/A lesson study-DC-past

      The teacher taught Ram the lesson.

(13) baccee-nee (aayaa-see) kapree pahn-ee

      child-agt nursemaid-instr clothes wear-past

      *The child wore clothes from the nursemaid.

      The child was dressed by the nursemaid.

(14) aayaa-nee baccee-koo kapree pahn-aa-yee

      nursemaid-agt child-D/A wear-DC-past

      The nursemaid dressed the child.

(15) raam-nee (naukar-see) khaanaa khaa-yaa

      Ram-agt servant-instr food eat-past

*Ram ate the food by the servant.

Ram was fed by the servant.

(16) naukar-nee raam-koo khaanaa khil-aa-yaa

servant-instr Ram-D/A food eat-DC-past

The servant fed Ram.

As (11)-(16) show, the contrast between transitives and their causatives is not in the number of agent arguments: both have an agent-1 that is the immediate performer of the action, as well as an agent-2, one degree of agency removed from the action of the verb. Thus, like the causative, the action of the noncausative transitive is also performed by an agent-2.

Semanto-syntactically, the transitive-causative contrast lies in subjectivization. The transitive subjectivizes agent-1, whereas the causative subjectivizes agent-2. As a semantic consequence, both the transitive (11) and the causative (12), for example, express the same fact, viz., that the teacher taught Ram. However, the transitive (11) is a statement from Ram's perspective, implying that Ram was the one who took the initiative in studying; the causative (12), on the other hand, is a statement from the teacher's perspective, implying that the teacher took the initiative in Ram's studying.

Thus, the transitive-causative pairs (11)-(16) show that minimally, the transitive-causative contrast is a subject contrast, not an extra-agent contrast.

3. A NEW GENERALIZATION

3.1 Interpretation of Data

The facts cited above show the GS account of
causativization to be highly unsatisfactory. The data shows
that an agent semantically equivalent to the causative agent
appears in noncausative sentences.[2] This means that first,
the current GS description of the causative agent as the
subject of the abstract verb CAUSE (under which the
noncausative is embedded) is unexplanatory; second, this
analysis must still find a satisfactory description for the
semantic equivalent of the causative agent in noncausative
sentences.

The data presented here point to a quite different
generalization: causatives merely foreground an agent that
may, but need not, occur in the corresponding noncausative
(where the syntactic realization of foregrounding is subject
status). This statement generalizes only on the subject
status of this agent, leaving open the option of its
presence (in languages like Hindi) or its absence (in
languages like English). Thus, this generalization on
causativization as a foregrounding mechanism expresses the
uniformity of causativization across languages, whether they

realize it as an extra agent contrast or merely as a subject contrast.

The data also make a second, incidental point. Since causative and noncausative case frames contrast minimally with respect to subject, it cannot be determined automatically, e.g., by a subject selection hierarchy (Fillmore 1977:80), which role in a given case frame will be subject. Rather, subject status will have to be specified in individual lexical entries. Using underlining to denote subject status, (17)-(25) provide some examples of minimally contrastive case frames.

(17) V, [Obj (Agt-1) __] vs. V, [Agt-1 Obj __]

    (18) kamraa (raam-see) put-aa

        Ram-agt room paint,Intr-past

        The room got painted (by Ram).

    (19) raam-nee kamraa poot-aa

        Ram-agt room paint,Tr-past

        Ram painted the room.

(20) V, [Agt-1 (Agt-2) __] vs. V, [Agt-2 Agt-1 __]

    (21) raam-nee (siitaa-see) nahaa-yaa

        Ram-agt Sita-instr bathe-past

        Ram bathed (with Sita's help).

    (22) siitaa-nee raam-koo nahl-aa-yaa

        Sita-agt Ram-D/A bathe-D/C-past

        Sita helped Ram bathe.

(23) V, [Agt-1 (Agt-2) Obj __] vs. V, [Agt-2 Agt-1 Obj __]

    (24) raam-nee (naukar-see) khaanaa khaa-yaa

        Ram-agt servant-instr food eat-past

      *Ram ate food from the servant.

      Ram was fed (by the servant).

    (25) naukar-nee raam-koo khaanaa khil-aa-yaa

        servant-instr Ram-D/A food eat-DC-past

      The servant fed Ram.

3.2 Support from Other Languages

Hindi is not an isolated example of a language defining causativization as subject contrast. Similar data are available from other languages. For example, the arbitrarily chosen Intr-Tr (3)-(4), 'The tree got cut by Ram' vs. 'Ram cut the tree', and the transitive-causative (11)-(12), '*Ram studied the lesson from the teacher' vs. 'The teacher taught Ram the lesson' can easily be replicated in the following Indian languages.[3]

Panjabi:

    (26) raam-koolõõ drakht kat-yaa

      Ram-by tree (subj) cut

    (27) raam-nee drakht kat-yaa

      Ram-subj tree cut

    (28) raam-nee maastar-koolõõ paath par-yaa

      Ram-subj teacher-by lesson studied

(29) maasṭar-nee raam-nuu paaṭh paṛ-aa-yaa

teacher (subj) Ram-dat lesson taught

Bengali:

(30) raam-ṭheekee gaac kaaṭ-lo

Ram-by tree (subj) cut

(31) raam gaac kaaṭ-lo

Ram (subj) tree cut

(32) raam maasṭar-ṭheekee paaṭh paaṛlo

Ram (subj) teacher-by lesson studied

(33) maasṭar raam-ṭheekee paaṭh paaṛaa-lo

teacher (subj) Ram lesson taught

Gujarati:

(34) raam-thii jaaṛ kapaayu

Ram-by tree (subj) cut

(35) raam-ee jaaṛ kaapyu

Ram (subj) tree cut

(36) raam-ee maasṭar-thii paaṭh vãã̃cyu

Ram (subj) teacher-by lesson studied

(37) maasṭar-ee raam-nee paaṭh vancaavãyu

teacher (subj) Ram-dat lesson taught

Telugu:

(38) raamuni vaalana komma tegenu

Ram by tree (subj) cut

(39) raamuḍu kommanu tencenu

Ram (subj) tree cut

(40) raamudu maastaru nunci paathamu neercenu

Ram (subj) teacher lesson studied

(41) maastaru raamuniki paathamu neerpenu

teacher (subj) Ram lesson taught

Also compare English 'I learned arithmetic from Mr. Jones' vs. 'Mr. Jones taught me arithmetic'.

4. EXPLANATORY APPEAL

An account of causativization in terms of subject contrast, implying foregrounding and backgrounding of roles, is more explanatory because it permits us to relate causative data to other areas of the grammar, where similar foregrounding and backgrounding of roles seem to be involved.

4.1 Intransitive-Passive

One advantage of describing causative contrast in terms of foregrounding and backgrounding of roles lies in our being able to capture the semanto-syntactic parallel of Tr-Intr pairs with Tr-passive pairs. This parallelism underscores the semanto-syntactic similarity of Intr sentences to passive sentences, thereby helping us to explain their striking formal similarity in Hindi grammar. (42) illustrates a Tr sentence, (43) its Intr counterpart, and (44) its passive counterpart.

(42) raam-nee peer kaaṭ-aa

Ram-agt tree cut,Tr-past

Ram cut the tree.

(43) (raam-see) peer kaṭ-aa/kaṭ gayaa

Ram-instr tree cut,Intr-past/cut,Intr comp verb

The tree (was/got) cut by Ram.

(44) (raam-see) peer kaaṭ-aa gayaa

Ram-instr tree cut,Tr-past comp verb

The tree was cut by Ram.

The Intr sentence (43), reminiscent of English
pseudopassives such as 'The book reads easily', is formally
and semantically similar to the passive construction
exemplified in (44). In fact, so close is their similarity
that Intr verbs have a well-respected history in Hindi
linguistics of being termed passive verbs (e.g., Sharma
1972:82-86). We can note three such similarities. (i) In
both the Intr and the passive sentences the agent is
optional and is marked by the instrumental c.m. -see. (ii)
The morpheme gayaa, which makes compound verbs out of simple
verbs, is required in all passive sentences. Although not
required in Intr sentences it facilitates interpretation,
especially if the Intr verb is not well established in the
language. For example, khay is a marginal Intr verb; as a
result, (46) is preferable to (45).

(45)?rooṭii khai-ii

bread eat,Intr-past

The bread (got/was) eaten.

(46) rooṭii khai gayii

bread eat,Intr comp verb

The bread (was/got) eaten.

(iii) Both the passive and the Intr constructions convey the semantics of ability. Thus, in addition to the glosses provided for (43) and (44), both sentences also imply that Ram had the ability to cut the tree.

Because of these similarities between the Intr and the passive, somewhere in the grammar we would like to regard the Intr and the passive as accomplishing the same results via different formal means. Given the semantic notions of foregrounding and backgrounding, we can regard the Intr and the passive as alternate means of foregrounding the patient and backgrounding the agent. The Intr accomplishes this through internal morphological change in the verb, whereas the passive accomplishes it through verb compounding.

Thus, analyzing causativization as subject contrast permits us to relate the Tr-Intr contrast to the Tr-passive contrast, and thereby to capture the similarity between Intr and passives.

4.2 Passive and Causative

Apparently, there are many similarities between causatives and passives that need to be expressed in the grammar. For example, in many languages it is felt that causative sentences causativize not the active but the passive of the corresponding noncausative. Thus, Grahame-Bailey (1950:58) makes this observation concerning the Hindi data: "There is no causal of the active voice of a transitive verb. The so-called causal is the causal of its passive. It means 'to cause the action of the transitive verb to be performed', not 'to make someone perform'".

Second, syntactically, many languages express the causee agent by the same c.m. used for the passive agent (Comrie 1976a:271).

Third, Masica (1976:75) notices that Gujarati uses the same form (-aa suffixation plus stem vowel shortening) for passivization that the closely related language Hindi uses for causativization--"a reminder that passives and causatives are phenomenan in the same semantic field and should be considered together."

To express the similarity between causative and passive agent phrases Comrie (1976a:271-275) considers an analysis that would passivize sentences before causativizing them, but points out many problems. However, given the

proposed   account   of   causative   contrast   in   terms   of
foregrounding and backgrounding of roles, an   analysis   that
actually   passivizes   sentences before causativizing them is
unnecessary.

We   noted   above that the passive (of transitives) and
the Intr are similar in two respects: both   foreground   the
patient   and   background   the   agent.   The   passive and the
causative (e.g., of transitives) are similar in at least one
respect: they   both background (i.e., de-subjectivize) the
agent-1.   The passive does so   because   it   foregrounds   the
patient,   and   the   causative does so because it foregrounds
agent-2.   As   a   result,   in   both   the   passive   and   the
causative,   the   agent-1   is de-subjectivized, backgrounded,
and deprived of initiative.   It is thus   understandable   why
the   noncausative proposition of causative sentences is felt
to be passive, and why the causee   agent   is   so   frequently
marked by the same c.m. as the passive agent.

4.3 Other Lexical Pairs

Highly similar phenomena to which causatives should be
related are the pairs of (47)-(50).

(47) I bought the book from John.

John sold me the book.

(48) I received the book from John.

John gave me the book.

(49) John obeyed the officer.

The officer commanded/instructed John.

(50) I borrowed the book from John.

John lent me the book.

Even though these pairs may intuitively be felt to be similar to causatives, current analyses of the latter make it difficult to relate them. For example, the CG model analyzes causatives as having an extra case category, Agent. The pairs of (47)-(50), however, do not show an extra-agent contrast. Similarly, the GS analysis involves an abstract verb CAUSE, and it is awkward[4] to analyze 'sell' as CAUSE TO BUY, 'give' as CAUSE TO RECEIVE, and 'command' as CAUSE TO OBEY.

However, given the analysis of causatives as involving subject contrast, the pairs of (47)-(50) can be seen to involve the same phenomenon. For example, 'buy' and 'sell' both refer to the same activity. In 'buy', however, it is the buyer who assumes control and initiative, whereas in 'sell' it is the seller who assumes control and initiative. Thus, we can say that formally, the lexical entries for 'buy' and 'sell' are different only in that 'buy' subjectivizes the buyer, whereas 'sell' subjectivizes the seller. Thus, the pairs of (47)-(50), like causative-noncausative pairs, involve subject contrast: this is the reason why the semantic contrast between the pairs of (47)-(50) is felt to be similar to the contrast between causatives and noncausatives.

To summarize: this chapter has presented counterexamples to the current view of causativization as an agent insertion mechanism, and has proposed an alternate view of causativization as a foregrounding/backgrounding mechanism. The new account is more explanatory because it permits us to relate causative data to other areas of the grammar that involve similar foregrounding and backgrounding of roles.

NOTES

*A modified version of this chapter was presented at the 1979 LSA Summer Meeting.

[1]C. Masica notes (pers. comm.) that one semantic correlate of the intransitive vs. transitive contrasts such as those in (3)-(8) that needs to be expressed is that between accidental vs. deliberate, volitional activity. This observation, if correct, would be predictable from the fact that the Intr have patient subjects, whereas Tr have agent subjects. By definition, patients do not have volition; the Intr events must therefore be interpreted as happening by themselves--if this is what Masica means by 'accidental'. Agents, however, have volition; they are responsible for the Tr events, so that these events are performed 'deliberately' by the agent. Since the contrast Masica notes is predictable from patient vs. agent status of the subject, it does not have to be accounted for separately.

[2]The presentation of counterexamples (3)-(8) and (11)-(16) has drawn two common responses. The first question raised is why the -see agent of the noncausatives in these pairs is analyzed as an agent, rather than, say, an

instrumental.

The answer is that no matter what label we give to this NP, the fact remains that it is semantically equivalent to the subject of the corresponding causative--the only semantic difference between these two NP's being accounted for by their subject vs. nonsubject status. Thus, calling one of these by a different name is merely avoiding the problem. Moreover, analyzing the -see NP in question as an instrumental has no other motivation than the desire to salvage an incorrect claim, and it is unintuitive. For example, instrumentals are elsewhere inanimates (and distinguished from agents on this basis). Attempting to follow through on this analysis makes it even messier. What happens to this 'instrumental' upon causativization? Does it just disappear? Do we need obviously ad hoc rules that change this 'instrumental' into a causative agent?

A second response that the counterexamples (3)-(8) and (11)-(13) draw is the question of why these pairs are analyzed as showing a causative-noncausative contrast rather than some other contrast such as subject-nonsubject. The answer here is that there is no independent criterion that would discount these pairs as causative vs. noncausative. Without such an independent criterion, the claim that causatives have an extra agent becomes circular and unfalsifiable: causatives have an extra agent, and if they do not have an extra agent, they are not causatives.

Furthermore, notice that the -see agent is optional in noncausatives. This means that if this optional agent is not realized, we get extra-agent contrast, but if this agent is realized, we get subject contrast--a rather flimsy basis for distinguishing two would-be different types of contrasts in the grammar.

[3]Mrs. Wadhwa, Shojal Mitra, Behroze Shroff, and Kumar Nadadur kindly supplied the Panjabi, Bengali, Gujarati, and Telugu data, respectively.

C. Masica notes (pers. comm.) that theekee in the Bengali data should be kee, and komma in the Telugu data should be cettu.

[4]As William Bright has pointed out (pers. comm.), a GS analysis for these pairs would be arbitrary, since there is no way of deciding whether 'buy', for example, is CAUSE TO SELL or whether 'sell' is CAUSE TO BUY.

4

CAUSEE AGENT CASE MARKING*

This chapter shows earlier analyses (Cole 1976, Comrie 1976a) of causee c.m. contrast to be inadequate and proposes an alternate account. It shows that the case markers -koo and -see correlate with the semantics affected vs. nonaffected, and that rules of the grammar consistently group these agents with other affected roles such as patients, datives, and experiencers.

1. INTRODUCTION

1.1 The Data

If the subject of the Base is an agent,[1] it has two c.m. possibilities in causee position. In this position, some agents must be marked by -koo, never -see.

    (1) raam-nee khaanaa khaa-yaa

        Ram-agt food eat-past

        Ram ate dinner.

    (2) mai-nee raam-koo/*see khaanaa khil-aa-yaa

41

I-agt Ram-D/A food eat-DC-past

I fed Ram.

(3) raam-nee nahaa-yaa

Ram-agt bathe-past

Ram bathed.

(4) mai-nee raam-koo/*see nahal-aa-yaa

I-agt Ram-D/A bathe-DC-past

I bathed Ram.

Other agents must be marked by -see, never -koo, as
illustrated by (5)-(8).[2]

(5) raam-nee peer kaaṭ-aa

Ram-agt tree cut-past

Ram cut the tree.

(6) mai-nee raam-see/*koo peer kaṭ-aa-yaa

I-agt Ram tree cut-DC-past,m

I made Ram cut the tree.

(7) raam-nee kapṛaa beec-aa

Ram-agt cloth sell-past

Ram sold the cloth.

(8) mai-nee raam-see/*koo kapṛaa bik-vaa-yaa

I-agt Ram cloth sell-IC-past,m

I had Ram sell the cloth.

Only a small handful of verbs (discussed in Section 4)
permit a choice between -koo and -see.

In   this   way,   causee c.m. provides a precise
classification of Hindi agents into two formal types: those
that upon causativization are marked by -koo, and those that
are marked by -see. Verb entries must therefore contain a
feature, which we can term [affected], such that agents of
verbs marked [+affected] will be signaled by the c.m. -koo
in causee position, those of verbs marked [-affected] will
be signaled by the c.m. -see, and those marked [±affected]
may be signaled by either -koo or -see.

Notice that patients, datives, and experiencers do
not need specification with respect to this feature because
they are automatically [+affected].

1.2 Previous Analyses

Two analyses have been advanced to account for causee
c.m. contrast, but these fail to account for Hindi data.

Comrie (1976a)   appeals   to   a   case   hierarchy
(Subject-Direct Object-Indirect Object-Other Oblique) to
determine causee c.m. By his analysis, subjects of
intransitive sentences should be marked by the Object c.m.,
while subjects of transitive sentences should be marked by
the Indirect Object c.m. Comrie points out, however, that
Hindi (along with several other languages) is an exception
to this claim. This is because causees such as those in (6)
and (8) should be marked by the dative c.m., there being no

other Indirect Object in the sentences; however, these causees 'skip' the dative c.m. to be marked instrumental (= Other Oblique). Thus, according to the case hierarchy account, the instrumental c.m. on these causees is a mystery. In addition, Comrie's account fails to explain why c.m. is used contrastively (see Section 4) on some causees.

In contrast to Comrie's syntactic criterion, Cole (1976) has proposed that c.m. contrast on the causee signals a semantic contrast. By his analysis, causees marked by the dative or accusative c.m. ought to be patients, whereas those marked by the instrumental c.m. ought to be agents. Hindi presents a counterexample to this hypothesis because many of the verbs that take -koo causees, e.g., the verbs for jump, run, get up, sit, eat, are obviously agentive verbs. In view of Cole's contention, however, the agent status of these causees needs better defense.

We can begin by noting that -koo causees fit the semantic description of agent as being "the typically animate perceived instigator of the action" (Fillmore 1968:24). Thus, the causee of the verb /pil-aa/ 'drink-DC' is the agent of the activity representeded by 'drink', the causee of /bhag-aa/ 'run-DC' is the agent of the activity represented by 'run'.

Second, many causatives have NP's other than -koo causees that must be analyzed as patients. Thus, in (2),

the NP khaanaa must be analyzed as patient.   Thus, if we
also analyzed raam-koo as patient, we would be violating the
Case Grammar constraint against having more than one
instance of the category patient in a single sentence.

Third, as subject (in the corresponding noncausative)
many of these agents [e.g., raam in (1) and (3)] are marked
by the subject-agent c.m., realized as -nee in the past.
Patient subjects are always marked -0, as in (9), and
experiencers are marked by -koo, as in (10).

> (9) raam piṭ-aa
>
>   Ram beat-past
>
>   Ram (got) beaten.
>
> (10) mujh-koo yah pasand hai
>
>   I-D/A this pleasing be
>
>   I like this.

Finally, as subjects, these agents can also take agentive
modifiers such as say kar kee, 'deliberately'.   This means
that if the -koo causees of (6) and (8) are to be
systematically related to the subjects of the corresponding
noncausatives (5) and (7), then these causees must be
analyzed as agents. Otherwise, ad hoc rules must change
noncausative agents to causative patients with some verbs.

There is indeed substance to Cole's observation that
causees marked instrumental are more agent-like than those
marked dative or accusative, but this is explained by the

hypothesis (to be developed) that in addition to their agent function, -koo causees also have a patient-like semantics of being affected by the verb activity.

The remainder of this chapter will be directed at establishing the semanto-syntactic difference between affected and nonaffected causee agents and to showing the affinity of affected agents to other affected roles such as patients, datives, and experiencers.

2. AFFECTED SEMANTICS

Affected and nonaffected agents are semantically differentiated by the semantics of being affected by the verb activity. This semantics should be associated with -koo causees because it permits us to make semantic generalizations on the distribution of the c.m. -koo.

The c.m. -koo primarily signals the dative, as in (11), and the patient, as in (12).

    (11) mai-nee siitaa-koo santaraa di-yaa

        I-agt Sita-D/A orange give-past,m

        I gave Sita an orange.

    (12) mai-nee siitaa-koo piiṭ-aa

        I-agt Sita-D/A beat-past,m

        I beat Sita.

Both datives and (the overwhelming number of) patients are clearly affected roles (as is evident in their label of direct and indirect object).

The semantics of being affected also relates to the use of -koo in dative subject constructions.[3] In such constructions, the subject is affected by the action without having control over it. One instance of this construction occurs with psychological predicates, as in (13).

(13) raam-koo gussaa aa-yaa

Ram-D/A anger come-past,m

Anger came to Ram. (= Ram got angry.)

(13) contrasts with (14), in which the subject, marked by -nee, is not affected and in control.

(14) raam-nee gussaa kar-aa

Ram-agt anger do-past,m

Ram showed anger

(without necessarily experiencing it).

Another instance of the subject being affected is when something is forced upon the subject, as in (15).

(15) raam-koo apnii kitaab parh-naa hai

Ram-D/A own book read-inf be,pres

Ram has to read his own book.

(15) contrasts with (16), where the subject is marked by -nee; in the latter the subject's volition is implied.

(16) raam-nee kitaab parh-ii

Ram-agt book read-past,f

Ram read the book.

The assorted instances of <u>NP-koo</u> presented above have a common, very specific semantics of being affected, being targets, being recipients, being acted upon. Thus, if we analyze the -<u>koo</u> causee agent as affected, it helps us preserve the semantic generalization associated with the distribution of the c.m. -<u>koo</u>. Without this notion, the distribution of -<u>koo</u> on some causees would be an exception to the semantic generalization on this case marking.

3. ENGLISH POSTVERBAL POSITION

The Hindi c.m. -<u>koo</u> finds its English counterpart in the postverbal object position; this position can be filled by objects, indirect objects, and experiencers, as illustrated by (17), (18), and (19), respectively.

(17) I wrote a letter.

(18) I wrote Mary a letter.

(19) John reminds me of my older brother.

Notably, this position can also be filled by affected causee agents in lexical (= single word) causatives, as illustrated in (20)-(21).

(20) I fed John some spaghetti. (= John ate spaghetti.)

(21) I walked Mary home. (= Mary walked home.)

Nonaffected agents cannot occupy the postverbal position via causativization: (22) and (23) are ungrammatical in the intended sense.

(22) *I built John a house. (= John built a house.)

(23) *I cut John a tree. (= John cut a tree.)

Thus, in English, too, a syntactic rule groups some agents with patients, datives, and experiencers; and the semantics of affectedness explains why this grouping is possible.

4. CONTRASTIVE CASE MARKING

A handful of verbs allow their causees to be marked by either the dative-accusative c.m. -koo or by the instrumental c.m. -see.

(24) mai-nee raam-see/-koo kitaab parh-vaa-ii

I-agt Ram-instr/-D/A book read-IC-past

I had Ram read the book.

(25) mai-nee raam-koo/-see masaalaa cakh-vaa-yaa

I-agt Ram-D/A/-instr spicing taste-IC-past

I had Ram taste the seasoning.

Other verbs in this category are /likh/'write', /gaa/ 'sing', etc.

The c.m. contrast on the causee signals a semantic contrast.   In   (24), when the causee agent of 'read-causative' is marked by -koo, the goal is to get the causee agent to read the book. When the causee agent is marked by -see, the goal is to get the book read, and the causee agent is merely an instrument to accomplish this end.

Similarly, when the causee agent of (25) is marked by -koo, the tasting is for his benefit, but when it is marked by -see, the tasting is for someone else's benefit. This semantic contrast is to be expected if the -koo, but not the -see causee is taken to be the affected agent.

5. SYNTACTICALLY GOVERNED COMPLEMENTARY DISTRIBUTION

With some causative verbs, the case markings -koo and -see are in what might appear to be syntactically governed complementary distribution. If the sentence has a patient, regardless of whether this patient is marked by -koo or -0, the causee agent is marked by -see. If, however, the sentence does not have a patient, the causee agent is marked by -koo. This is illustrated in (26)-(39).

(26) mai-nee raam-see saamaan uth-vaa-yaa

I-agt Ram-instr luggage get up-IC-past

I had Ram lift/carry the luggage.

(27) mai-nee raam-koo uth-vaa-yaa

I-agt Ram-D/A get up-IC-past

I had Ram get up.

(28) mai-nee raam-see saamaan nikal-vaa-yaa

I-agt Ram-instr luggage come out-IC-past

I had Ram take the luggage out.

(29) mai-nee raam-koo nikal-vaa-yaa

I-agt Ram-D/A come out-IC-past

I had Ram come out.

These sentences show that the causee agent is the target of the verb activity when it is marked by -koo, but not when marked by -see. Thus, even this apparent syntactic distribution is captured by the proposed semantic generalization.

6. SEMANTIC COMPLEXITY

-koo causees can be interpreted as very patient-like. For example, (30) would be appropriate if raam were a baby or an invalid, and was literally picked up.

(30) mai-nee raam-koo uṭh-aa-yaa

I-agt Ram-D/A get up-DC-past

I made Ram get up./I picked Ram up.

However, a totally agentive interpretation is also always available. Thus, (30) would be equally appropriate if I merely told Ram to get up, and he performed the act of getting up on his own.

Similarly, (31) would be appropriate if I spoonfed Ram.

(31) mai-nee raam-koo khil-aa-yaa

I-agt Ram-D/A eat-DC-past

I fed Ram./I made Ram eat.

However, (31) would be equally appropriate if I merely

served Ram his dinner, and he did the eating unassisted.

Clearly, the traditional distinction between the categories <u>agent</u> and <u>patient</u> is not linguistically available in this position. Thus, representation of this NP as either agent or patient alone would be arbitrary. However, its representation as a semantically complex unit <u>affected</u> <u>agent</u> would explain why such divergent readings are possible.

7. LEXICALIZATION

Because semantically the -<u>koo</u> causee is partly like a patient, -<u>aa</u>-suffixed causatives with affected causees potentially invite reanalysis as a single activity in which the causative agent is the subject and the causee the object in a quasi-transitive verb. By contrast, because the nonaffected causee is not like a patient, these same causatives with nonaffected causees cannot be conceptualized as a single activity.

Conceptualization as a single activity paves the way for lexicalization, i.e., the development of idiosyncrasy. Such idiosyncratic semantics typically identifies a specific activity by means of which the causative agent affects the causee agent. As a result, causative semantics cannot be described literally in terms of the noncausative semantics, and additional information is needed to specify the

activities to which these causatives refer.   (32) shows some
such common causatives.

> (32) paṛh-aa
>
> teach
>
> ≠CAUSE TO STUDY
>
> khil-aa
>
> babysit
>
> ≠CAUSE TO PLAY
>
> khil-aa
>
> feed
>
> ≠CAUSE TO EAT
>
> ṭhahr-aa
>
> provide temporary lodgings
>
> ≠CAUSE TO WAIT
>
> sun-aa
>
> narrate
>
> ≠CAUSE TO LISTEN
>
> man-aa
>
> cajole
>
> ≠ CAUSE TO AGREE

By contrast, the nonaffected causee yields only literal
causative semantics;   e.g., /kaṭ-aa/ 'have cut', /bin-aa/
'have knit'.

Thus, we can generalize: the relation between the causative agent (of an -aa-suffixed verb) and an affected causee leads to lexicalization of causative semantics, whereas the relation between the causative agent (of an -aa-suffixed causative verb) and a nonaffected agent causee does not lead to such lexicalization.

Shibatani (1975:94) claims that causatives can be viewed as a single activity only if the causee is in a patient role. Consequently, he claims (1975:95, 96) that Hindi /daur/ 'run' and English 'run' and 'dance', which have agentive causees, do not lead to single events. This claim is not true for either the Hindi or the English examples. Counterexamples are Hindi /daur-aa/ 'chase', English 'I ran/chased him out of the house', 'I danced her around the room'. These sentences show that Shibatani's generalization on patients must be extended to include affected agents.

8. CAUSATIVE IMPLICATION

Only causatives with affected agents tolerate the negation of their noncausative, as in (33).

(33) mai-nee raam-koo haṭ-aa-yaa par vah nahĩĩ haṭ-aa

I-agt   Ram-D/A   move-DC-past,m   but   he   not

move-past,m

I (tried to) move Ram, but he didn't move.

(33) is possible because of the dual nature of the koo

agent as both an affected entity and an agent or performer.
As a result, the causative clause of (33) can be interpreted
as making a statement about the affected status of the
causee without saying anything about its volitional status,
whereas the noncausative clause makes a statement about its
volitional status; thus, despite their seeming contradiction
they are compatible.

Causatives with nonaffected causees, on the other
hand, never permit negation of their noncausative.

(34)*mai-nee raam-see peer̥ kat̥-aa-yaa par us-nee nahı̃ı̃

kaat̥-aa

I-agt Ram-instr tree cut-DC-past,m but he-agt not

cut-past,m

I made Ram cut the tree but he did not cut it.

-see causees have only agent or performer status

consequently, negation of the corresponding noncausative
represents a contradiction in (34).

Thus, the semantics of affectedness is needed to
define a necessary condition on causees before the reading
of (33) is permitted; furthermore, this semantics explains
why such readings become permissible.

9. UNSPECIFIED OBJECT DELETION

Only causatives with an affected agent may undergo unspecified object deletion.

(35) mai-nee raam-koo paaṭh/ϕ paṛh-vaa-yaa

I-agt Ram-D/A lesson/ϕ read-IC-past

I had Ram read (the lesson).

(36) mai-nee raam-koo gaanaa/ϕ ga-vaa-yaa

I-agt Ram-D/A song sing-IC-past

I had Ram sing (a song).

Causatives with nonaffected agents do not undergo unspecified object deletion (unless, of course, the object is specified in the immediate discourse context).

(37) mai-nee raam-see peeṛ/*ϕ kaṭ-vaa-yaa

I-agt Ram-instr tree cut-IC-past

I had Ram cut the t́ree.

(38) mai-nee raam-see makaan/*ϕ ban-vaa-yaa

I-agt Ram-instr house build-IC-past

I had Ram build the house.

Thus, causatives must have an affected role in surface structure, whether as a patient or an affected agent.

10. DIRECT AND INDIRECT CAUSATIVE CONTRAST

The -aa form signals direct, contactive causation only
if the verb has an affected agent; such an -aa form
contrasts with the corresponding -vaa form which always
signals indirect, noncontactive causation. This is
illustrated by the pairs of (39)-(42).

(39) mai-nee larkee-koo parh-aa-yaa

I-agt boy,obl-D/A study-DC-past,m

I taught the boy.

(40) mai-nee larkee-koo parh-vaa-yaa

I-agt boy,obl-D/A study-IC-past,m

I had the boy study.

(41) mai-nee larkee-koo khil-aa-yaa

I-agt boy,obl-D/A eat-DC-past,m

I fed the boy.

(42) mai-nee larkee-koo khil-vaa-yaa

I-agt boy,obl-D/A eat-IC-past,m

I had the boy eat.

(39) and (41) represent contactive causation, while the
corresponding (40) and (42) represent noncontactive
causation.

The -aa form does not signal contactive causation if
the verb has a nonaffected agent, i.e., it signals

noncontactive causation, just like the corresponding -vaa form.

 (43) mai-nee naaii-see baal kaṭ-aa/vaa-yee

   I-agt barber-instr hair cut-DC/IC-past,m pl

   I had the barber cut (someone's) hair.

 (44) mai-nee naukar-see kaam kar-aa/vaa-yaa

   I-agt servant-instr work

   I had the servant do work.

Thus, an affected agent forms a necessary condition for contactive causation and a nonaffected agent a sufficient condition for noncontactive causation. Furthermore, the distinction between these agents is crucial in predicting when the -aa and -vaa forms will be semantically contrastive, and when noncontrastive with respect to contactive vs. noncontactive causation. (The significance of the affected agent in the formation of contactive vs. noncontactive causation in Hindi and other languages is discussed more fully in Ch. VI.)

 To conclude: the case markers -koo and -see on the causee agent correlate with the semantics affected and nonaffected, and rules of the grammar consistently link affected agents with other affected roles such as patient, dative, and experiencer.

NOTES

*A modified version of this paper was presented at the 1978 LSA Winter Meeting.

[1] Non-agent causees are marked either by the c.m. -koo or by the c.m. -0. Both -koo and -0 signal affected causees, and as such contrast with the c.m. -see, which signals nonaffected causees. The semantic difference between -koo and -0 causees will not be of concern to us here; it is part of a more general semantic contrast associated with these c.m. units, and is discussed at length in Saksena 1980.

[2] The starred version of sentence (8) is ungrammatical only in the intended sense. It would be perfectly grammatical with Ram as a dative, with the translation 'I had the cloth bought for Ram'.

[3] The dative subject NP would be classified as a subject because (i) it occupies the leftmost position in the SOV order of Hindi sentences, and (ii) it is the antecedent of the possessive reflexive, as in (15).

5

THE AFFECTED AGENT*

The distinction between affected and nonaffected
agents made in Chapter IV is also significant in noncausee
position, i.e., when these agents are the subjects of Base
sentences. Rules similar to those discussed in Chapter IV
distinguish affected from nonaffected agents in Base
sentences and group the former with other affected roles
such as patients, datives, and experiencers.

Formally, the affected agent can be defined equally
precisely in Base sentences. In these sentences, affected
agents are those which in corresponding causatives are
realized with the c.m. -koo; nonaffected agents are those
which are realized with the c.m. -see.

1. SEMANTIC DIFFERENCE

(1) shows a sampling of verbs that take affected
agents (i.e., those marked by -koo in the corresponding
causative).

(1) /deekh/ 'see, look'; /pii/ 'drink'; /bhaag/ 'run

away'; /siikh/ 'learn'; /dauṛ/ 'run'; /caṛh/

'climb'; /kuud/ 'jump'; /ghuum/ 'go out'; /jhuul/

'swing'.

These agents share a common semantics. The agents of such

verbs   are   also   the   recipients   of   the verb activity and

constitute   the   target   toward   which   this   activity   is

directed.   Thus, the activities represented by eat and read

are not only directed at their objects (e.g., food or book),

but   also   toward   their   agents.   Frequently, these agents

undergo a change of state physically (as in the activity of

running)   or   psychologically   (as   in   the   activity   of

studying).   In other words, these agents have some of the

properties   that   one   typically expects of patients.   These

agents are   not   only   do-ers   (i.e.,   performers   of   their

activities) but   also   do-ees   (i.e.,   recipients   of   these

activities).¹

     (2)   shows   a   sampling of verbs that take nonaffected

agents.

     (2) /phaaṛ/ 'tear'; /mããj/ 'scour'; /phĩĩc/ 'wash';

        /kar/ 'do'; /puuch/ 'ask';   /khool/   'open';

        /ḍhaak/   'cover something';   /ḍhuur/ 'look for';

        /boo/ 'plant'; /rakh/ 'put'.

The   agents   of   (2)   are in sharp contrast to the agents of

(1). The activities of (2) are directed only at their

patients, not   their   agents.²   As   a result, the agents of these activities are not affected, are not recipients, and do not undergo a change of state.

2. REFLEXIVE VERBS

Readers unfamiliar with Hindi may have trouble comprehending how subjects of the intransitives run, walk, get up, sit, etc. can be viewed as being affected by the verb activities. However, the claim finds independent syntactic support in French and Spanish, where Hindi verbs with affected agents are typically realized as reflexive verbs.[3] (3)-(4) give examples from French, (5)-(6) from Spanish.

> (3) Marie sè lève à huit heures.
>
> Marie (subj) reflexive get up at eight o'clock
>
> Marie gets up at eight o'clock.
>
> (4) Marie s'assoit sur le sofa.
>
> Marie (subj) reflexive sits on the sofa
>
> Marie sits on the sofa.
>
> (5) Ahora me acuesto.
>
> Now reflexive lie-down,I
>
> Now I am going to lie down.
>
> (6) 'Levántense todos!
>
> Get up, reflexive everybody
>
> Get up, everybody!

Also compare English 'I fed myself some rice', 'I sat myself down on the couch'.

3. AGENT ADVERBIALS

    Only affected agents may occur in conjunction with a
-see adverbial agent, and this -see phrase is interpreted as
an agent that acts upon the affected agent.

        (7) raam-nee maastar-see parh-aa

            Ram-agt teacher-instr study-past,m

            Ram studied with the teacher.

        (8) raam-nee naukar-see khaanaa khaa-yaa

            Ram-agt servant-instr food eat-past,m

            Ram ate with the servant('s help).

With some affected agents, a -see agent may appear odd.

        (9) raam siitaa-see cal-aa

            Ram Sita-instr walk-past,m

            Ram walked with Sita('s help).

In order to be appropriate, sentences such as (9) require
the assumption that their subjects are invalids, infants,
machines, or toys, needing help from another agent in order
to perform such a basic function as walking.

    By contrast, nonaffected agents do not permit being
acted upon by a -see agent.

        (10)*raam-nee siitaa-see peer kaat-aa

            Ram-agt Sita-instr tree cut-past,m

            Ram cut the tree with Sita's help.

Thus, the semantics of affectedness describes a necessary condition restricting agents that can appear with an agent adverbial, and distinguishes agents which may take agent adverbials from those which may not.

In this respect, too, the -koo agent displays its recipient, +affected, patient-like behavior. This is because patient and experiencer subjects also occur in conjunction with -see agents, and the semantic relation between these NP's is parallel: the -see agent acts upon or affects the patient and the experiencer. (11) illustrates such a -see phrase with a patient subject and (12) illustrates one with an experiencer subject.

(11) peer raam-see kaṭ-aa

tree Ram-instr cut,Intr-past,m

The tree (got) cut by Ram.

(12) raam siitaa-see ḍar-aa

Ram Sita-instr fear-past

Ram (got) scared by Sita.

Thus, the notion of affected, shared by patients, experiencers, and affected agents, provides the semantic basis and thereby the explanation for the grouping of these roles.

4. CONSTRAINT ON ENGLISH LEXICAL CAUSATIVES

Since only affected agents can occupy the post-verbal position in English (Chapter IV.3), this condition defines a constraint   on   the   formation   of English lexical (= single-word) causatives: only those (agentive) verbs that have affected agents yield corresponding lexical causatives, as in (13)-(14).

(13) John ran out. $\longrightarrow$ I ran John out.

(14) John bathed. $\longrightarrow$ I bathed John.

Furthermore, gaps in the lexicon are often filled in child-language, and in dialectal and idiolectal variation. For example, (15) was uttered by a child whose mother had been swinging her around on the dance floor.

(15) Mommy, please dance me again.

(16) was used by a child who was afraid of being dropped.

(16) Oh, don't fall me!

(17) was used by a lady whose husband had rejected several empty seats in a picnic ground.

(17) Well, where do you want to sit us?

Thus, if English lacks lexical causatives for verbs with affected agents, that lack only represents an accidental gap in the grammar.

By contrast, we do not get English lexical causatives for (noncausative) verbs with nonaffected agents; we are forced to use causatives with 'make' and 'have'.   Thus,

'John did some errands' must be causativized as 'I had/made John do some errands', not *'I did John some errands'; 'John cut a tree' must be causativized as 'I had John cut a tree', not *'I cut John a tree'. Thus, English causative verbs with nonaffected agents are systematic gaps in the lexicon.

5. UNSPECIFIED OBJECT DELETION

The generalization on unspecified object deletion associated with causatives that have affected causees (Chapter IV.9) can be extended to noncausatives with affected agents. (18)-(19) show that the subjects of (20)-(21) are affected agents, and these noncausatives can undergo unspecified object deletion.

   (18) mai-nee raam-koo vahãã gaanaa ga-vaa-yaa

         I had Ram sing a song there.

   (19) mai-nee raam-koo paaṭh paṛh-aa-yaa

         I taught Ram the lesson.

   (20) raam-nee vahãã gaanaa/ϕ gaa-yaa

         Ram-agt there song/ϕ sing-past

         Ram sang (a song) there.

   (21) raam-nee paaṭh/ϕ paṛh-aa

         Ram-agt lesson/ϕ read-past

         Ram read (the lesson).

The c.m. -see on the causees of (22)-(23) shows that the

noncausatives (24)-(25) involve nonaffected agents; as a result, these noncausatives cannot undergo unspecified object deletion.

(22) mai-nee raam-see peer̤ kat̤-vaa-yaa

I had Ram cut a tree.

(23) mai-nee raam-see kapṟaa bik-vaa-yaa

I had Ram sell the cloth.

(24) raam-nee peer̤/*φ kaat̤-aa

Ram-agt tree cut-past

Ram cut the tree.

(25) raam-nee kapṟaa/*φ beec-aa

Ram-agt cloth sell-past

Ram sold the cloth.

Thus, extending the distinction between affected and nonaffected agent to noncausative agents allows us to generalize the rule of unspecified object deletion to noncausatives as well.

6.   INTRANSITIVE GENERALIZATION

Subjects of intransitive sentences are typically patients, as in (26).

(26) peer̤ kat̤-aa

tree cut-past,m

The tree (was) cut.

They may also be experiencers, as in (27).

    (27) raam câûk-aa

        Ram startle-past,m

        Ram (was) startled.

Importantly, they can also be agents.

    (28) raam daur-aa

        Ram run-past,m

        Ram ran.

    (29) raam uth-aa

        Ram get up-past,m

        Ram got up.

    (30) raam nahaa-yaa

        Ram bathe-past,m

        Ram bathed.

(31)-(33) show that the agents of (28)-(30) take the c.m. -koo upon causativization and are, therefore, affected agents.

    (31) mai-nee raam-koo daur-vaa-yaa

        I had Ram run.

    (32) mai-nee raam-koo uth-vaa-yaa

        I had Ram get up.

    (33) mai-nee raam-koo nahl-vaa-yaa

        I had Ram bathed.

Nonaffected agents do not appear as intransitive subjects.

    Thus, the semantics of affectedness is needed to

describe agents that can be intransitive subjects and to

distinguish them from those which cannot.   Second, the

semantics of affectedness, common to all   intransitive

subjects--patients,   experiencers,   and   the   relevant

agents--provides the semantic basis for this syntactic slot.

Since intransitive subjects are all affected roles, Comrie's

finding that intransitive subjects are marked by the   direct

object c.m.   upon causativization was to be expected.

    Notice that it is now possible to merge the

generalization on   intransitives with the generalization on

unspecified object deletion.   Since intransitives as well as

transitives   must have an affected role, one can say that an

affected role (patient, experiencer, or agent) is a required

element of every Hindi sentence, transitive or intransitive.

In this sense, affected roles are more basic in the   grammar

than nonaffected roles (e.g., instrumentals, nonaffected

agents, causative agents).[4]

    To the extent that the subject of the intransitive,

like the object of the transitive, is always an affected NP,

the semantics of affectedness may provide the semantic basis

of ergativity.   A wrinkle may be added to this analysis,

however, because the subjects of some transitives, such as

those for _eat_ and _read_, are also affected.   It would

therefore be interesting to see how ergative languages treat

these transitives.   Notice that in Hindi these verbs

function as pseudo-intransitives (Section 5).

7. SIGNIFICANCE

The distinction between affected and nonaffected agents in Base sentences is theoretically significant. It is customary in current linguistics to regard the notion agent as a unified semanto-syntactic category that is fundamentally distinct from other categories such as patient. Case Grammar has explicitly claimed that case categories such as agent and patient represent the fundamental semanto-syntactic units and distinctions in the grammar. The existence of the affected agent calls this view into question in three ways.

First, the notion agent is not a single semanto-syntactic category, because agents fall into two formally distinct types, the affected and the nonaffected. Second, the distinction between case categories is not clear-cut, because the semantics of being affected by the verb activity links some agents semantically and syntactically to categories such as patients, datives, or experiencers. Finally, since case categories can be classified as either affected (patients, datives, experiencers, affected agents) or nonaffected (nonaffected agents, instrumentals, causative agents), the affected-nonaffected contrast is clearly more fundamental

and   primitive   than   that   of   the   case   categories   it
encompasses.

      To   conclude: this   chapter   has   shown   that   the
distinction between affected and nonaffected   agents   is   as
significant   in   noncausatives   as   it   is   in   causative
sentences.   These agents are distinguished by a   variety   of
semanto-syntactic   rules   which   consistently group affected
agents with other affected roles such as patients,   datives,
and experiencers.

NOTES

*A modified version of this chapter was presented at
the 1979 LSA Winter Meeting.

Zide 1972 has used the term 'affected' for Gorum, but
the phenomenon she discusses seems to be a different one.
First, her classification is different because in her
analysis many intransitive subjects (such as those of 'run
away, escape') are -affected, as are the subjects of
transitives such as 'see' and 'eat'. Second, the claims she
makes for these verbs--that affected verbs do not have
corresponding transitives (or First causatives) and that
there can be only one affected participant per sentence--are
not only different, but incompatible with those of this
paper.

Masica (1976.III) notices a subclass of transitives
viz. eat, drink, hear, understand, learn and read, that he
labels 'ingestives' because they have the common semantic
property of "taking something into the body or mind
(literally or figuratively)". The membership of (verbs
with) affected causees is much larger. These verbs are not
restricted to transitives, since they include all
intransitives as well; they are not restricted to agents,
since they also include patients and experiencers; they are
not restricted to ingestives, since they also include the

agents of <u>daur</u> 'run', <u>cal</u> 'walk', <u>likh</u> 'write' etc, which cannot be characterized as "taking something into the body or mind". Rather the proposed classification corresponds more closely to the grouping of intransitives and a special subclass of transitives that shows up repeatedly in Masica's cross-linguistic data.

[2]One reader points out that many of the agents I have classified as nonaffected are affected at least to the extent that they expend energy. Another critic notes that the agent of 'sell', here shown to classify as nonaffected, is affected physically, in that the seller receives money, as well as psychologically, in that the seller is happier at having struck a deal. With some use of the imagination, similar questions could be raised about other agents.

Note, therefore, that Chapters IV and V rely on an extremely precise definition of the notion <u>affected</u> <u>agent</u>, viz., case marking in causee position, and they provide many syntactic correlates which agree with the c.m. criterion--thus yielding a grammatically well-defined set of agents. Furthermore, in addition to the criterion of agent semantics (Section 1) that these critics are questioning, these chapters also provide many independent semantic arguments (e.g. Chapter IV.2, 3, and 5) for why the semantics of affectedness should be linked with one set of

agents. These arguments are further confirmed by the
constant grouping in both Chapters IV and V of the affected
agent with other affected roles such as patient, dative, and
experiencer. Thus, the semantic properties of affected
agents serve to indicate what the grammar considers relevant
to the semantics of affectedness. In other words, even if
the properties mentioned by these critics are indeed
affecting properties, the grammar clearly does not consider
them so.

Incidentally, notice that the property of expending
energy mentioned by the first critic characterizes all
agents, affected and nonaffected. Since this property
already forms part of the definition of agents, it is
understandable why it would not count again in their further
classification as affected vs. nonaffected.

[3]C. Masica (pers. comm.) points out that many of these
have taken on idiosyncratic connotations: e.g., /ir/ 'go,
walk', /irse/ 'go away'; /comer/ 'eat', /comerse/ 'eat up'.

[4]The affected agent is always subject of the Base (or
causee of the corresponding causative), never a derived
agent, e.g., the subject of -aa and -vaa causatives. In
this sense, too, the affected agent is more basic than the
nonaffected agent.

6

CONTACT IN CAUSATION*

The distinction between contactive and noncontactive causation shows up repeatedly in languages (Masica 1976: Ch III, Cole 1976), and is claimed by the prestigious Xolodovič 1969 (according to Comrie 1976b:481) to be "fundamental" in their description. Arguing against earlier descriptions, this chapter provides an alternate analysis of this important contrast.

0. INTRODUCTION

The difference between contactive and noncontactive causation can be illustrated with -aa vs. -vaa causatives. One important property distinguishing them is that noncontactive -vaa causatives may contain one or more occurrances of an intermediary agent, as in (1)-(2), but contactive -aa causatives such as (3) may not do so.

   (1) mai-nee (maasṭar-see) raam-koo paṛh-vaa-yaa

       I-agt teacher-instr Ram-D/A read-IC-past

       I had the teacher make Ram study.

(2) mai-nee (siitaa-see) (raam-see) (naukar-see) peer
    kat-vaa-yaa

    I-agt Sita-instr Ram-instr servant-instr tree
    cut-IC-past

    I had Sita make Ram make the servant cut the tree.

(3) mai-nee (*maastar-see) raam-koo parh-aa-yaa

    I-agt teacher-instr Ram-D/A study-DC-past

    I taught Ram (*through the teacher).

In addition, causers of noncontactive causatives may
be physically absent from the causative activity, as in (4),
whereas causers of contactive causatives, as in (5), may not
be so absent.

(4) mai-nee larkee-koo khil-vaa-yaa aur mai tab tak
    ghuum aa-yaa

    I-agt boy,obl-D/A eat-IC-past,m and I meanwhile
    around go-past

    I had the boy eat and meanwhile I went for a
    walk.

(5)*mai-nee larkee-koo khil-aa-yaa, aur tab tak mai
    ghuum aayaa

    I-agt boy,obl-D/A eat-DC-past,m and meanwhile I
    around go-past

    I fed the boy and meanwhile I went for a walk.

1. EARLIER ANALYSES

Despite the prevalence of the contactive-noncontactive contrast in languages, it has not been dealt with in much detail in the general theoretical literature; moreover, there are two major misconceptions in this area. First, earlier grammars attribute this contrast to an intermediary; and, second, they treat the notion of contact as a single, unanalyzable semantic concept. These views make earlier analyses problematic.

1.1 An Intermediary

Prevalent Analysis: In the general literature, the contrast between contactive and noncontactive causation has been explained in terms of an intermediary. For example, this is the position of Xolodovič 1969, summarized in Masica (1976:55):

> causation may be principally of two kinds, "distant" and "contactive". In the latter the agent does something to the object, bringing about the new condition by direct contact; in the former he makes use of an intermediary agent, and serves only as the "instigator" of the act.

Masica bases his areal, cross-linguistic investigation on this theoretical premise, adopting Xolodovic as his "guru-pioneer" because "the theoretical spadework of the Kholodovich group is quite thorough" (Masica 1976:54). In fact, he goes a step further to claim (1976:55) a socio-linguistic basis for the intermediary and resulting noncontactive causation. Talking about these causatives, he says:

> Their frequency and pervasiveness probably depends less on universal norms than on the degree of social differentiation and functional specialization developed in a given society. This is a statement that seems to apply happily to Indian society but needs to be tested against, or have its terms carefully defined in terms of, "primitive" societies...

In Hindi linguistics too, a similar explanation in terms of an intermediary is offered for the -aa vs. -vaa causatives, which are labelled variously as direct vs. indirect (Balachandran 1973:17), contactive vs. distant (Masica 1976:54), Transitive vs. Causative (Pray 1970), and, most commonly, as First vs. Second Causative (Kachru 1966, Kellogg 1972, Sharma 1972, Masica 1976). Regardless of their terminological preferences, these grammars all claim that -vaa forms are 'double causatives', in a causative relation to -aa forms; and as such, the subject of the latter is realized as an intermediary[1] (Kachru 1966, Balachandran 1973:17, Kellogg 1972:252, Masica 1976:49) in the former. These claims can be supported with pairs such as (6)-(7) where the subject of the contactive (6) is semantically equivalent to the intermediary of the noncontactive (7).

(6) raam-nee makaan ban-aa-yaa

Ram-agt house build-DC-past

Ram built a house.

(7) mai-nee raam-see makaan ban-vaa-yaa

I-agt Ram-instr house build-IC-past

I had Ram build a house.

Theoretically,   the   claim   that   noncontactives   are
'double   causatives'   containing   an   intermediary   is
significant   because   it   presents   an   argument   for   a
transformational analysis which derives noncontactives   from
an   embedding   of   the   corresponding   contactives   under an
abstract verb CAUSE.   Such an analysis provides   an   elegant
formalization   of   the   traditional   notions   'First'   and
'Second'   causation   by   equating   them   with   degrees   of
causative embedding.

Counterarguments: Despite the widespread use of   this
analysis,   explaining   the difference between contactive and
noncontactive causation in terms of an   intermediary   and/or
repeated causation is incorrect.

First, the intermediary is always an optional, never a
required   expansion   in   noncontactives.   Thus,   (8)   is   a
noncontactive that does not have an intermediary overtly.

(8) mai-nee laṛkee-koo doo bajee khil-vaa-yaa

I-agt boy,obl-D/A two o'clock eat-IC-past

I had the boy eat at two o'clock.

(8) could be used, for example, if I, as a boss kept the boy
busy till two o'clock, and let him go for lunch then.

As a corollary, such noncontactives do not necessarily imply the corresponding contactives. Thus, (8) does not automatically imply (9), and (10) does not automatically imply (11).

(9) kisii-nee larkee-koo doo bajee khil-aa-yaa

someone-agt boy,obl-D/A two o'clock eat-DC-past,m

Someone fed the boy at two o'clock.

(10) mai-nee baccõõ-koo (garmiyõõ-bhar) (har-rooz)

(doo ghantee) parh-vaa-yaa

I-agt children,obl-D/A summer-entire every day

two hours study-IC-past,m

I had the children study (two hours) (every day) (for the entire summer).

(11) kisii-nee baccõõ-koo (garmiyõõ -bhar) (har rooz)

(doo ghantee) parh-aa-yaa

Someone-agt children-D/A summer-entire every day

two hours study-DC-past,m

Someone taught the children (two hours) (every day) (for the entire summer).

It would therefore be incorrect to posit the intermediary (and contactive causation) as part of the semantics of noncontactive causation.

Second, noncontactives without intermediaries still contrast with their corresponding contactives, as in (12)-(15).

(12) mai-nee larkee-koo parh-vaa-yaa

I-agt boy,obl-D/A study-IC-past,m

I had the boy study.

(13) mai-nee larkee-koo parh-aa-yaa

I-agt boy,obl-D/A study-DC-past,m

I taught the boy.

(14) mai-nee larkee-koo daur-vaa-yaa

I-agt boy,obl-D/A run-IC-past,m

I had the boy run.

(15) mai-nee larkee-koo daur-aa-yaa

I-agt boy, obl-D/A run-DC-past,m

I chased the boy.

Consequently, analyses that rely on the concept of an intermediary fail to explain the semantic contrast involved in the pairs of (12)-(15).

This contrast can be appreciated by focusing on an actual DC-IC pair such as parh-aa 'teach' and parh-vaa 'have (s.o.) study'. Contactive causation in the former is achieved by the act of teaching, which puts the causative agent into direct psychological contact with the causee agent. Noncontactive causation in the latter can be achieved by using an intermediary such as a tutor but in a variety of other ways as well: the causative agent could put the causee agent into school, pay his tuition, provide him with books or study time, promise a reward, or merely lock him into a cubicle--anything that may contribute to the causee agent's studying. Thus, although the intermediary no doubt represents a common means of accomplishing indirect causation in the real world, it is only one of many available options. Hence, it cannot be considered a necessary condition of noncontactive causation.

That it is not a sufficient condition either has been seen in (3), where we found that inserting an intermediary in a contactive causative does not make it a noncontactive causative, only an ungrammatical one; and other conditions (to be specified in Section 2.2) must be met.

To conclude, the intermediary is not a signficant feature of contactive causation: the semantics of noncontactive causation is unaffected regardless of whether sentences contain zero, one, or more occurrences of the intermediary [as in (8), (1) and (2), respectively].

1.2 Single, Unitary Semantic Notion

A second misconception found in earlier grammars is that causative contact comprises a single, unitary semantic notion, not permitting further analysis. Because of this assumption, earlier grammars associate contactive (= First) causation with the suffix -aa, and noncontactive (= Second) causation with the suffix -vaa.

This analysis is problematic because many -aa forms do

not signal the expected semantics of contactive causation;

rather, they signal noncontactive causation, just like the

corresponding -vaa forms: e.g., /kaṭ-aa/, /kaṭ-vaa/ 'have

cut'; /kar-aa/, /kar-vaa/ 'have do'. These doublets pose an

embarrassing puzzle in causative description.

Many grammarians (e.g., Kellogg 1972) do not mention

these mergers at all; others note them only in the few

paradigms which fail to achieve the three-way schema of

these grammars--as in the typically cited example /kar/ 'do'

vs. /kar-aa/, /kar-vaa/ 'have do'.

When they do notice these mergers, grammarians often

take a prescriptive way out. For example, talking about the

verb /kar/ 'do' which produces a merger, Sharma (1972:116)

has this to say:[2]

> Its second causal form /kar-vaa/ is (unfortunately) in
> existence, but is identical in meaning with the first
> causal /kar-aa/. Many such "false" second causals are
> in common use. They have, in fact, been formed on the
> analogy of "true" second causals (like /paṛh-vaa/,
> /gir-vaa/ etc.), and should be treated as mere
> alternative forms (which had better be discarded) of
> the first causals.

These grammars (cf. Kachru 1966:64) treat such mergers

as morphological alternates, begging the question why they

occur. Since the problem is most obviously morphological,

modern linguists find it particularly easy to dismiss. For

example, in a series of sections devoted to Hindi

causatives, Shibatani (1975:39) says the problem why all -aa

causatives do not behave alike is "... a good illustration of the fact that analyses that are based on a purely morphological consideration ... are not adequate to account for linguistic phenomena"; and Masica (1976:51) says these 'irregular' causatives are part of the inevitable "asymmetries of the system".

This paper shows that these morphological problems can be avoided if the notion of contact is regarded as a semntic composite rather than a single semantic unit.

2. A PROPOSAL

2.1 Contact as a Semantic Composite

The notion of contact in causatives and elsewhere can be considered a semantic composite, it being a sum of contact initiation and contact completion. Initiation and completion, furthermore, can be stated as conditions on the parties involved.

To take an example outside causatives, consider John's contacting Mary by phone. In order to initiate contact, John must dial Mary's number, and in order to complete the contact, Mary must pick up the phone. Given these conditions, John will be able to contact Mary by phone only if John dials Mary's number and Mary picks up the phone. John will not be able to make contact if either John does not dial Mary's number or Mary does not pick up the phone.

Thus, in order for contact to take place, John and Mary must fulfill the conditions that constitute contact initiation and completion, respectively.

In a parallel manner, contact in causation too can be described as a sum of contact initiation and completion, and these components can be stated as conditions on the relevent parties, viz., the causer and the causee.

2.2 Significant Conditions

The conditions for causative contact can be stated as follows: in order for causative contact to be initiated, the causer must be personally involved in the verb activity; and in order for causative contact to be completed, the causee must be the target of this activity.

The generalizations of causer involvement and causee affectedness are morphologically explicit in Hindi. Using the term causer to refer to the subject of -aa and -vaa causatives, a personally involved causer is signaled by the suffix -aa on the verb, whereas a noninvolved causer is signaled by the suffix -vaa on the verb. Using the term causee for that NP in these causatives that corresponds to the subject of the Base, affected causees are marked by the dative and accusative c.m. -koo (or -0), and nonaffected causees by the instrumental c.m. -see (Chs. IV, V).

It is useful to recall from Chapters IV-V that

affected   causees   correspond   to   the   subject   of   all
intransitives as well as a special subclass of transitives
(such   as   eat,   drink,   study,   etc.), and that these can be
patients, experiencers, as well as   a   special   subclass   of
agents.   All   of   these   roles   have   the   common   semantic
property of being target recipients of the verb activity.

2.3 Predictions

A two-way contrast on the causer and the causee yields
four possible combinations, as displayed in (16).

(16)

	+involved causer -aa	-involved causer -vaa
+aff causee -koo	-aa/-koo	-vaa/-koo
-aff causee -see	-aa/-see	-vaa/-see

The   concept   of   contactive   causation   requires   both   an
involved   causer   and   an   affected   causee.   Of   the   four
combinations of (16), only one, viz., -aa/-koo   meets   that
requirement;   as such, it is the only combination signalling
contactive causation.   The other three combinations lack one
or   both   of   the   requirements;   as such, they alike signal
noncontactive causation.

Associating contactive causation   only   with   the
-aa/-koo combination,   and noncontactive causation with the
other three is exactly   what   the   data   calls   for,   as   is
verified in the following section.

3. VERIFICATION

3.1 Contactive-Noncontactive Semantics

The   proposed   analysis   is   descriptively   adequate
because   it   correctly   identifies   causatives   which convey
contactive causation, and separates them from those which do
not.

Correlation with Suffix Contrast: The analysis claims
that the suffixes -aa and -vaa correlate with contactive vs.
noncontactive causation when they   have   causees   marked   by
-koo   (or   -0).   This   can   be   verified   in   intransitive
paradigms such as (17)-(19) and (20)-(22).

(17) makaan ban-aa

house build-past

The house (got) built.

(18) mai-nee makaan-koo/0 ban-aa-yaa

I-agt house (-D/A) build-DC-past

I built a house.

(19) mai-nee makaan-koo/0 ban-vaa-yaa

I-agt house (-D/A) build-IC-past

I had a house built.

(20) raam uṭh-aa

Ram get up-past

Ram got up.

(21) mai-nee raam-koo uṭh-aa-yaa

I-agt Ram-D/A get up-DC-past

I made Ram get up.

(22) mai-nee raam-koo uṭh-vaa-yaa

I-agt Ram-D/A get up-IC-past

I had Ram get up.

It can also be verified with transitive paradigms such as (23)-(25) and (26)-(28).

(23) raam-nee paaṭh paṛh-aa

Ram-agt lesson read-past

Ram read the lesson.

(24) mai-nee raam-koo paaṭh paṛh-aa-yaa

I-agt Ram-D/A lesson read-DC-past

I taught Ram the lesson.

(25) mai-nee raam-koo paaṭh paṛh-vaa-yaa

I-agt Ram-D/A lesson read-IC-past

I had Ram read the lesson.

(26) raam-nee khaanaa khaa-yaa

Ram-agt food eat-past

Ram ate dinner.

(27) mai-nee raam-<u>koo</u> khaanaa khil-<u>aa</u>-yaa

I-agt Ram-D/A food eat-DC-past

I fed Ram dinner.

(28) mai-nee raam-<u>koo</u> khaanaa khil-<u>vaa</u>-yaa

I-agt Ram-D/A food eat-IC-past

I had Ram eat dinner.

Thus, the proposed analysis explains why the suffixes -<u>aa</u>
and -<u>vaa</u> do correlate sometimes with contactive vs.
noncontactive causation.

<u>No</u> <u>Correlation</u> <u>with</u> <u>Verbal</u> <u>Suffixes</u>: The proposed
formulation claims that the suffixes -<u>aa</u> and -<u>vaa</u> alike
signal noncontactive causation when they have causees marked
by -<u>see</u>. This can be illustrated in the paradigms (29)-(30)
and (31)-(32).

(29) naaii-nee baal kaaṭ-ee

barber-agt hair cut-past

The barber cut (someone's) hair.

(30) mai-nee naaii-<u>see</u> baal kaṭ-<u>aa</u>/<u>vaa</u>-ee

I-agt barber-instr hair cut-DC/IC-past,m pl

I had the barber cut (someone's) hair.

(31) naukar-nee kaam kar-aa

servant-agt work do-past,m

The servant did (some) work.

(32) mai-nee naukar-<u>see</u> kaam kar-<u>aa</u>/<u>vaa</u>-yaa

I-agt servant-instr work do-DC/IC-past,m

I had the servant do work.

Thus, the proposed definition explains why the suffixes -<u>aa</u> and -<u>vaa</u> do not sometimes signal the contrast between contactive and noncontactive causation, thereby accounting for the major puzzle in their description.

The discussion of the contactive vs. noncontactive contrast makes clear that every sentence that conveys noncontactive causation must contain either a noninvolved causer or a nonaffected causee, and either of these conditions are sufficient in creating noncontactive causation. As such, there is no need to mention an intermediary in stating the range of contactive vs. noncontactive causation.

3.2 Minimal Semantic Contrasts

The proposed analysis serves not only to delineate the range of contactive vs. noncontactive causation, but also helps explain minimal semantic contrasts associated with the relevant suffixes and c.m.

<u>Minimal Verbal Suffix Contrast</u>: Minimal suffix contrast is illustrated by sentences such as (30) and (32), repeated below as (33) and (34).

(33) mai-nee naaii-see baal kaṭ-aa/vaa-yee

   I-agt barber-instr hair cut-DC/IC-past,m pl

   I had the barber cut (someone's) hair.

(34) mai-nee naukar-see kaam kar-aa/vaa-yaa

   I-agt servant-instr work do-DC/IC-past,m

   I had the servant do work.

Even though the -aa and the -vaa forms of (33) and (34) alike signal noncontactive causation, there is nevertheless a shade of difference in their meanings. Masica's (1976:48) informant ventured that the -aa form is specialized for instances where the causative agent wanted his hair cut or his work done (as opposed to someone else's hair or work), but the author here feels that this causee agent could also be personally helping or supervising the action. The appropriate generalization therefore seems to be that the -aa type of causative agent is, in some way, personally involved in the action. The notion of a 'personally involved causer' posited for the -aa suffix helps explicate such intuitions about these -aa forms elegantly. Earlier analyses (e.g., Kachru 1966:64) which treated the -aa and -vaa versions of (33)-(34) as morphological alternates have no way of explaining this systematic shade of meaning difference.

   Minimal C.M. Contrast: Minimal c.m. contrast is illustrated in (35) and (36).

(35) mai-nee raam-<u>koo</u>/-<u>see</u> kitaab paṛh-vaa-ii

I-agt Ram- book read-IC-past

I had Ram read the book.

(36) mai-nee raam-<u>koo</u>/-<u>see</u> masaalaa cakh-vaa-yaa

I-agt Ram- spicing taste-IC-past

I had Ram taste the seasoning.

Chapter IV has already discussed the semantic correlates of this contrast. In (35), when the causee agent of 'read-causative' is marked by -<u>koo</u>, he is the psychological recipient of the activity expressed by reading. When this agent is marked by -<u>see</u>, the causee is not a target--since the goal now is to get the book read, and the causee is a means (e.g., in a secretarial capacity) toward this end. Similarly, when the causee agent of (36) is marked by -<u>koo</u>, the goal is to get the causee to taste the seasonings, but when this agent is marked by -<u>see</u>, the goal is to get the seasonings tasted (e.g., to see if they need correcting) and the causee is a means towards this end. Thus, the -<u>koo</u> but not the -<u>see</u> type of causee is the recipient of the verb activity. In this way, the definition of contactive causation in terms of affected vs. nonaffected causees provides a sensitive semantic description of the -<u>koo</u> vs. -<u>see</u> contrast on causees.

To summarize: the proposed analysis accounts for a whole range of semantic data by using the same general terms

of causer involvement and causee affectedness. It accounts
for the range of contactive vs.   noncontactive causation,
and within this, for fine shades of meaning differences on
causers and causees.   Significantly, these semantic
generalizations are in a one-one relationship with
morphological generalizations, and there are no
"asymmetries" that earlier linguists found in this regard.

   With these demonstrations all aspects of the proposed
analysis have been verified.

4. A CROSS-LINGUISTIC PERSPECTIVE

   An analysis of contactive causation in terms of an
involved causer and an affected causee is explanatory for
other languages as well.[3]

4.1 Affected Causee

   (i) Data: One set of languages yield only contactive
causatives as simple verbs (= not involving overt
embedding), and in these languages such causative formation
is restricted to intransitives and a special subset of
transitives.   For example, Armenian yields causatives with
intransitives as well as some transitives; e.g., /hish/
'remember' vs. /hishecn/ 'remind', /ut/ 'eat' vs. /utecn/
'feed'; /kem/ 'drink' vs. /kemecn/ 'give drink to'. Arabic
yields causatives from intransitives--e.g., /birik/ 'kneel'

vs. /birrik/ 'make s.o. kneel', as well as some transitives--e.g., /fihim/ 'understand' vs. /fahham/ 'make understand'. Greek verbs can be used transitively or intransitively (similar to English 'walk,intr' vs. 'walk,tr'), and transitives such as /matheno/) can be interpreted as either the transitive 'learn' or the causative 'teach'. In English, only intransitives and a subclass of transitives yield lexical causatives, e.g., 'die' vs. 'kill', 'eat' vs. 'feed', 'learn' vs. 'teach'.

Analysis: Section 2.2 specified that contactive causatives are restricted to affected (rather than nonaffected) causees; in addition, it equated affected causees as corresponding to the subject of all intransitives and a special subset of transitives. It becomes expected, then, why the contactive causatives of these languages should be restricted to this particular set of verbs.

(ii) Data: In a second set of languages, the causative suffix yields contactive causation with intransitives and a special class of transitives, but indirect causation with other transitives. Such is the case of the -AA in Bengali, Oriya and Assamese. For example, Bengali yields contactives with intransitives, e.g., /jal/ 'burn' - /jal-aa/ 'light, kindle' and some transitives, e.g., /paṛ/ 'study' - /paṛ-aa/ 'teach' but noncontactives with other transitives, e.g., /kar/ 'do' - /kar-aa/ 'have

do'.   In Telegu, we get contactives with some transitives,
e.g., /tinu/ 'eat' - /tinipincu/ 'feed', but   noncontactives
with other transitives, e.g., /kaṭṭu/ 'build' - /kaṭṭ-incu/
'have build'.

Analysis: Section 2.2 claimed the affected causee to
be a necessary condition of contactive causation, and the
nonaffected   causee   to   be   a   sufficient   condition   for
noncontactive causation.   In addition, it equated the
affected causee with the subject of all intransitives as
well as a special subset of transitives, and the nonaffected
causee with the subject of other transitives.   Thus, if we
assume that the causative suffix in these languages
signifies causer involvement, it would be completely
expected why this suffix would yield contactive causatives
with one set of verbs, and noncontactive causatives with
another set of verbs.   In fact, its behavior would be
exactly parallel to that of the -aa suffix in Hindi--which
yields contactives with intransitives and a subset of
transitives, and noncontactives with another set of
transitives.

(iii) Data: A third set of languages include Quechua,
Kannada, and Hungarian, which according to Cole (1976) yield
direct causation with causees marked by the dative or
accusative c.m., and indirect causation with causees marked
by the instrumental c.m. Cole illustrates his contention

with data such as (36)-(41).

Bolivian Quechua:

(36) nuqa Fan-ta rumi-ta apa-či-ni

I Juan acc. rock acc. carry-cause-1psg

I made Juan carry the rock.

(37) nuqa Fan-wan rumi-ta apa-či-ni

I Juan instru. rock acc. carry-cause-1 psg

I had Juan carry the rock.

Kannada:

(38) Avanu nanage bisketannu tinnisidanu

he-nom me-dative biscuit-acc. eat-cause-past

He fed me a biscuit.

(39) Avanu nanninda bisketannu tinnisidanu

he-nom me-instru. biscuit-acc eat-cause-past

He caused me to eat a biscuit.

Hungarian:

(40) Köhögtettem a gyereket.

I-caused-to-cough the boy-acc.

I made the boy cough.

(41) Köhögtettem a gyerekkel.

I-caused-to-cough the boy-instru

I had the boy cough. (by asking him to do so)

Analysis: Again, section 2.2 defined an affected

causee as a necessary condition of contactive causation, and

the nonaffected causee as a sufficient condition of
noncontactive causation.   In addition, it identified
affected causees as those marked by the dative or accusative
c.m., and nonaffected causees as those marked by the
instrumental c.m. Thus, if we assume that the causative
suffix in these languages signifies an involved causer, it
is completely predictable why this suffix should yield
contactive causatives with causees marked by one type of
c.m., but noncontactives with causees marked by another type
of c.m.   In fact, this suffix would be seen to behave
exactly like the Hindi suffix -aa, which yields contactives
with causees marked by the dative or accusative c.m., and
noncontactives with causees marked by the instrumental c.m.

To conclude, the role of the affected causee in
creating the semantics of contactive causation in other
languages is exactly what we would expect on the basis of
Hindi data. In this way, the analysis of contactive vs.
noncontactive causation in terms of an affected causee
provides an explanation for a range of cross-linguistic
data, rendering them systematic and predictable.

4.2 Involved Causer

Since existing grammars do not describe causative
semantics in terms of causer involvement, one does not
expect to find this notion in existing grammars of other
laguages; however, current descriptions are suggestive.

Section 2.2 identified the semantics of causer involvement as the second essential ingredient of contactive causation; in addition, it equated the contrast of causer involvement vs. noninvolvement with contrastive causative suffixes. Notice, then, that many languages yield contrastive causative suffixes that partake in the formation of contactive vs. noncontactive causation. Moreover, as with Hindi, existing grammars typically describe these suffixes as marking First vs. Second causation. Among the Indian languages, such suffixes are found in Panjabi and Nepali (-AAW vs. -WAAW), Gujarati (-AAW vs. -(A)AḌAAW), Kashmiri (-AAV vs. -AAVɨNAV), Marathi (-AW vs. -AWAW), and Sindhi (-AA vs. -RAA). Outside of the Indian subcontinent, contrastive suffixes can be found in Turkish (-DİR/T vs. repeating an allomorph), Kachen, a Tibeto-Burman language (prefix SI vs. suffix SI), Burmese (aspirating initial consonant vs. suffix -ZEI), Ethiopian (-A vs. -AS), possibly Swahili (-ZA/YA vs. ESHA), and Tswana (-SA vs. -ISA). Among the European languages we find them in Georgian (A-EB vs. A-INEB), Lithuanian and Latvian (-IN vs. -DIN), Hungarian (-ET vs. -TET), and Finnish (-TA vs. -TUTTA).[4]

Thus, it seems likely that as with Hindi, contrastive suffixes in these languages too, carry not the generalizations of First and Second causation, but those of causer involvement vs. noninvolvement.

5. PARAMETERS IN THE DEVELOPMENT OF CAUSATIVE SYSTEMS

Languages do not need the mechanism of two contrastive causative suffixes to express the contrast between contactive and noncontactive causation: they can do so with only a single suffix. For example, lexical causatives can be used to express contactive causation, while a regular suffix expresses noncontactive causation. Or, (as with the languages presented in (ii) and (iii) of 4.1 above,) a single suffix can signal contactive causation with affected causees, and noncontactive causation with nonaffected causees. The question then arises: why do languages such as Hindi develop a two-suffix mechanism to express what other languages can express with a single suffix? The Hindi example provides insight.

This language has severe lexical and syntactic restrictions which prevent contrastive use of c.m. [as in (32) and (33)] to any significant extent. First, (as discussed in Ch. V.1) the choice of c.m. -koo vs. -see on the causee is lexically severely constrained. Most verbs permit only -koo causees (e.g., /khaa/ 'eat', /dauṛ/ 'run', /pii/ 'drink', etc.), or only -see causees (e.g., /kaaṭ/ 'cut', /bin/ 'knit', /beec/ 'sell', etc.), and only a small handful (e.g., /paṛh/ 'study') allow causee c.m. to contrast.

Second, choice of c.m. is further restricted because
of a c.m. constraint (Saksena 1980.II) such that Hindi
simplexes, including causatives, favor only one instance of
the c.m. -koo per sentence. To illustrate, the causative
sentence (42) may mark its causee with either -koo or -see.

    (42) mai-nee harkaaree-koo/-see citthii likh-vaa-ii

        I-agt scribe-D/A/instr letter write-IC-past

    I had the scribe write a letter.

If, however, the sentence were to also contain a dative
(which must be marked by -koo), then the causee would
obligatorily be marked -see, as in (43).

    (43) mai-nee harkaaree-see/*-koo siitaa-koo citthii

          likh-vaa-ii

        I-agt   scribe-instr/*D/A   Sita-D/A   letter

        write-IC-past

    I had the scribe write a letter to Sita.

In short, the possibility of using c.m. contrastively is
severely restricted. Thus, if the distinction between
contactive and noncontactive causation were to rely on c.m.
alone, this contrast would be similarly restricted. The
suffixes -aa and -vaa therefore take the burden of signaling
contactive vs. noncontactive causation from the marginal
c.m. contrast by introducing the (contactive vs.
noncontactive) distinction on all verbs that can take -koo

causees. This is the major advantage of having a two-suffix system.

However, this system changes because of two factors. First, these suffixes fail to achieve the contactive-noncontactive contrast on verbs with -see causees (section 2), so that the dual suffix mechanism is wasted on the many -see verbs in the language, producing the redundant, wasteful -aa vs. -vaa 'morphological alternates'--a highly undesirable state of affairs. In these mergers, because the latter forms signal noncontactive causation consistently, they are preferred (see Chapter VII, fn. 2) to the -aa form, thus setting in motion the gradual demise of the latter choice.

Second, the remaining -aa forms (which express contactive causation) display increasing lexicalization (Chapter IV.7, Chapter VIII). In combination, these two tendencies pave the way for a system that will contain a limited set of lexical -aa causatives and a regular and productive set of -vaa causatives.

Once -vaa is left as the only regular and productive causative suffix, it will probably be reanalyzed as the unmarked causative suffix, i.e., one signifying an involved causer; and once the reanalysis takes place, this suffix will signal contactive causation with causees marked by the dative or accusative c.m., and noncontactive causation with causees marked by the instrumental c.m.--so that c.m. will now become the sole determiner of contactive vs. noncontactive causation [as with the languages of (36)-(41)]. In other words, the Hindi system would then resemble the present-day Japanese system, which has a set of lexical causatives and a set of productive causatives; and within the latter, a direct, contactive vs. indirect, noncontactive contrast correlating with c.m. contrast.

Thus, the proposed analysis of contactive vs. noncontactive causation provides important parameters in the development of causative systems, and tracing this development enables us to relate the systems of different languages.

To conclude: the notion of contact in causation must be analyzed as a semantic composite of the more primitive notions of causer involvement and causee affectedness, to coincide with morphological generalizations. These notions are able to separate causative types conveying contactive causation from those conveying noncontactive causation; they help capture minimal semantic contrasts associated with c.m. and verbal suffixes in Hindi as well as other languages; and they provide the dimensions for language change in this area.

NOTES

*A modified version of this and the following chapter were presented as a colloquium titled "A Semantic Typology of Causatives" at the 1980 Winter Meeting of the Linguistic Society of America. Bernard Comrie, David Dowty, and Larry Horn served as discussants.

[1]Despite the popularity of this term, the intermediary is seldom defined, and the task does not appear simple either. The problem is to find a definition for this notion which includes Ram in (i) below (because it signals noncontactive causation) but excludes Ram in (ii) (because it signals contactive causation).

    (i) mai-nee raam-see makaan ban-vaa-yaa

       I had Ram build a house.

    (ii) mai-nee raam-koo paaṭh paṛh-aa-yaa

       I taught Ram the lesson.

If the intermediary is defined as mediating between two agents, it will not cover 'Ram' in (i); if it is defined as mediating between an agent and an object, it will also include 'Ram' in (ii).

    Of course, the obvious difference between the two instances of 'Ram' in (i)-(ii) is their c.m.; however, this difference cannot be used in defining the intermediary because in these grammars, c.m. itself is to be predicted on the basis of notions such as 'intermediary'. In that the term 'intermediary' cannot be defined independently of noncontactive causation, earlier grammars involve circularity: an intermediary is determined from noncontactive causation, and noncontactive causation is determined by an intermediary.

Edith Moravcsik has suggested (pers. comm.) that it is possible to define the intermediary from the point of view of a given action, such as building the house in (i); given this action, a person is an intermediary if he carries out this action without at the same time initiating it: such a definition would cover Ram in (i) but not in (ii).

However, this suggestion merely shifts the arbitrariness to a different level. For example, as Ch. I.3 noted, a noncontactive causative such as /dikh-vaa/ can be glossed as 'have (something) seen', 'have (someone) see', or 'have (someone) show'; thus, there is no automatic procedure for deciding which of these several actions should be singled out as the basis for determining an intermediary.

[2]I have Romanized Sharma's examples, which are cited in the Devanagari script.

[3]Much of the cross-linguistic data here, as well as in

Ch. VII.3 can be found in Masica 1976.III.

    [4]The following are some sample illustrations:

Kashmiri:
        /con/ 'to drink'
        /caavun/ 'to give drink to'
        /caavɨnaavun/ 'have someone give drink to'

Marathi:
        /bas/ 'sit'
        /basaw/ 'seat'
        /basawaw/ 'cause to seat'

Sindhi:
        /virch/ 'be weary'
        /virchaa/ 'weary'
        /virchaaraa/ 'cause to weary'

Ethiopian:
        /läffaa/ 'be soft'
        /aläffaa/ 'soften'
        /asläffa/ 'cause to soften'

Tswana:
        /tlala/ 'become full'
        /tlatsa/ 'fill'
        /tladisa/ 'cause to fill'

Finnish:
        /kulke/ 'go'
        /kuljetta/ 'bring'
        /kuljetutta/ 'bring with someone's help'

Hungarian:
        /ég/ 'burn, intr'
        /éget/ 'burn, tr'
        /égettet/ 'have burned by someone'

Japanese:
        /waku/ 'boil, intr'
        /wakasu/ 'boil, tr'
        /wakasaseru/ 'have boil'

7

A SEMANTIC MODEL
OF PARADIGMATIC CONTRASTS

Traditional and theoretical studies, both language-specific and language-universal, have hitherto described causative semantics with notions such causative vs. noncausative, and First vs. Second causative--notions which are relative, and which do not carry any absolute, constant semantic value. This chapter argues that causative paradigms must be analyzed using a model that includes a set of absolute semantic parameters.

1. INTRODUCTION

1.1 The Proposed Semantic Model

Causative paradigms can be classified by the set of four semantic parameters schematized in (1).

(1) Model   Examples

   I [Obj __]   ka̪t 'cut, intr'

   II [Agt (Obj) __]   dau̪r 'run', ban-aa 'make'

   III [Agt Agt (Obj) __]   pa̪rh-aa 'teach'

   IV [Agt Agt (Obj) __]   pa̪rh-vaa 'have study'

106

In this schema, I represents an intransitive, objectival
verb, whereas II is an agentive verb, transitive or
intransitive (irrespective of whether it is morphologically
simple or derived). III is a 'double transtive', and both
II and III are contactive causatives. IV is a noncontactive
causative, regardless of whether it is a transitive or a
double-transitive, for this distinction is not sigificant in
noncontactives (see 1.3).

The slur connecting NP's in II and III is a notation
expressing contactive causation, the slur with a cross in IV
expresses noncontactive causation. The parentheses around
the object mean that the frame in question can be
illustrated by either a verb that has an object or one that
does not (and not that the object is optional with the verbs
that illustrate these frames).

The universal significance of the contactive vs.
noncontactive contrast has been documented in Chapter VI,
and the contrast between objectival/intransitive vs.
agentive/transitive is well established enough not to need
additional elaboration.

1.2 Motivation

A Derivation

Hindi provides an example of a language with a
well-developed derivational mechanism. The derivational

rules (presented in Chapter I.1) can be reviewed here briefly.

Base verbs may take a suffix -aa and a suffix -vaa; and if this Base verb has a long stem vowel and transitive syntax, it will also yield a corresponding short-stem vowel intransitive. These rules account for a four-way possible paradigm such as the one for 'cut': /kaṭ/ - /kaaṭ/ - /kaṭ-aa/ - /kaṭ-vaa/.

The subject of intransitive and a special subclass of transitive Bases is indicated as +affected in the verb entry (in order to trigger the c.m. -koo in the corresponding causative); with these verbs -aa suffixation yields a direct, contactive causative. The subject of other transitive Bases is indicated as -affected in verb entries (to trigger the c.m. -see in the corresponding causative); with these verbs -aa suffixation results in an indirect, noncontactive causative. -vaa suffixation, on the other hand, results in an indirect, noncontactive causative with all verbs.

Earlier Analysis

Earlier studies have described causative semantics using relative, derivational notions such as 'causative' vs. 'noncausative', and 'First' vs. 'Second' causative. The former set of terms are probably well familiar to the general linguist; the latter set are used in universal grammars   such   as   Xolodovič   1969   (according   to   Masica   1976:

Ch III),   as well as language-specific grammars such as those

for   Hindi.   The   latter   include both traditional (Kellogg

1972, Sharma 1972) as well as modern, formal studies (Kachru

1971,   Kleiman 1971) which equate the notions of 'First' and

'Second' with degrees of causative embedding.

Semantically, the notions (First/Second) causative and

noncausative are imprecise, and do not   carry   any   constant

semantic   value.   For   example,   an   actual noncausative may

have either frame I (e.g., /kaṭ/ 'cut, intr'),   or   frame   II

(e.g.,   /khaa/   'eat'); and   an   actual   causative can have

either frame II (/ban-aa/ 'make'), III (/paṛh-aa/   'teach'),

or IV (/paṛh-vaa/ 'have study').

Similarly,   a   First   causative   formed   from   an

intransitive   verb   will yield a transitive (frame II) which

is semantically no different from noncausative   transitives.

In   addition,   if   First   causation applies to a verb marked

+affected   subject,   it   will   yield   a   contactive   causative

(frame   II   or   III);   but   if   it   applies to a verb marked

-affected   subject, it will yield a   noncontactive   causative

(frame IV).

Thus,   the   notions   (First/Second)   causative   vs.

noncausative do not signify any unique semantic (i.e., case

frame) value, making it surprizing why they have been

considered descriptively adequate so long, and so widely in the literature.

Clearly, generalizations about the semantic composition of verbs need to be abstracted from actual verbs, and the model (1) does precisely that.

1.3 Prerequisites of Contactive Causation

The notion of contact in causation was developed in Chapter VI, and its salient features can be reviewed here briefly.

Contactive causatives such as /ban-aa/ 'make', /haṭ-aa/ 'move' from intransitive Bases, and /paṛh-aa/ 'teach', /khil-aa/ 'feed' from transitive Bases imply physical and psychological contact between the causer and the causee. Noncontactive causatives such as /ban-vaa/ 'have made', /haṭ-vaa/ 'have move' from intransitive Bases, and /kaṭ-aa/ 'have cut', /bik-aa/ 'have sell' from transitive Bases do not involve contact between the causer and the causee.

Contactive causatives crucially require two conditions. They must have both an involved causer and an affected causee; if either of these conditions is not met, i.e., if either the causer is -involved or the causee is -affected, we get noncontactive causation.

In Hindi, the causative suffix -aa signals an involved causer while the suffix -vaa signals a -involved causer; the

c.m. -koo (or 0) signals an affected causee, while the c.m.
-see signals a -affected causee. This analysis accounts for
why only the c.m. and suffix combination -aa/-koo signals
contactive causation, whereas the other three combinations
-aa/-see, -vaa/-koo, -vaa/-see alike signal noncontactive
causation.   Thus,   in   (2)-(5), only (2) signals contactive
causation, and (3)-(5) alike signal noncontactive causation.

Contactive:

(2) mai-nee raam-koo paath parh-aa-yaa

    I-agt Ram-D/A study-DC-past

    I taught Ram the lesson.

Noncontactive:

(3) mai-nee raam-koo paath parh-vaa-yaa

    I-agt Ram-D/A lesson study-IC-past

    I had Ram study the lesson.

(4) mai-nee raam-see kaam kar-aa-yaa

    I-agt Ram-instr work do-DC-past

    I had Ram do work.

(5) mai-nee raam-see kaam kar-vaa-yaa

    I-agt Ram-instr work do-IC-past

    I had Ram do work.

As (2)-(5) show, the -aa and -vaa forms are contrastive only
if they have affected causees marked by -koo, as in (2) vs.
(3), but noncontrastive (with respect to contactive vs.
noncontactive causation) if they have nonaffected causees

marked by -see, as in (4)-(5).

Finally, recall from Chs. IV-V that affected causees correspond to the subjects of all intransitives and a special subset of transitives, whereas nonaffected causees correspond to the subject of other transitives. In addition, affected causees can be equated with those marked by the dative or accusative c.m., nonaffected causees with those marked by the instrumental c.m.

This chapter will now proceed to show the explanatory value of model (1), first for Hindi grammar, and then for universal grammar.

2. EXPLANATORY VALUE FOR HINDI

Positing (1) as a semantic model for Hindi paradigms explains a variety of problems in this area.

2.1 Upper Bounds

A transformational model (Kachru 1966, 1971; Kleiman 1971) derives Hindi paradigms by successive applications of a causative transformation; there is nothing in this framework to stop this transformation from being infinitively recursive. However, the causative process in Hindi has strict upper bounds: paradigms can have no more than four possible members. In other words, we have no explanation for why the causative process ceases to be

morphologically expressed after a certain number of stages,
and why this number happens to be four.

However, with the abstract paradigm (1) as a model,
the problem of stopping a potentially recursive process does
not arise. This model stipulates in advance that languages
can have a maximum of only four contrastive members. As
such, paradigms with four contrasts are possible, as in (6),
but none with more.

(6) Model   Actual Paradigm

   I [Obj ___]   /dikh/ 'get seen'

   II [Agt Obj ___]   /deekh/ 'see, look'

   III [Agt Agt Obj ___]   /dikh-aa/ 'show'

   IV [Agt Agt Obj ___]   /dikh-vaa/ 'have see/shown'

The four-way semantic contrast of the paradigm for 'see,
look' coincides with the case frames of the four-way model
paradigm.

Thus, model (1) explains why Hindi can have as many
as, but never more than four members in the causative
paradigm.

2.2 Idiosyncratic Number of Contrasts

Paradigms that have the maximum number of four semantic
contrasts are rare; typically, they show three or fewer
contrasts. It would appear then, that the data is rather
erratic in this respect.   As a result, earlier grammars

present many verb/paradigm classifications according to the number of contrasts these involve. However, model (1) renders this aspect of the data quite systematic.

This model makes available an extremely valuable notion--that of semantic gaps in an actual paradigm (for contrasts permitted by the model). Such gaps result if the prerequisites for a semantic contrast specified by the model are not met in the derivation of an actual paradigm.

Since Hindi has a full derivational mechanism, systematic gaps in this language arise due to lexical restrictions (rather than derivational restrictions). Lexical restrictions typically create gaps for III, I, or both, as discussed below.

Gap for III: Contactive causation in case frame III [of (1)] requires an affected causee (1.3). Thus, if a verb does not have an affected subject, -aa suffixation will not be able to create a contrast III; rather, we get a semantic gap for this frame. This results in a three-way semantic contrast, even though the paradigm utilizes the maximum possible four-way morphological, derivational mechanism.

(7) Model   Actual Paradigm

    I [Obj ___]   /kaṭ/ 'get cut'

    II [Agt Obj ___]   /kaaṭ/ 'cut'

    III [Agt Agt Obj ___]   ---

    IV [Agt Agt Obj __]   /kaṭ-aa/-/kaṭ-vaa/ 'have cut'

Because /kaaṭ/ 'cut' in (7) does not have an affected agent,
/kaṭ-aa/ and /kaṭ-vaa/ are semantic doublets, both
signifying noncontactive causation. In this way, the
predictable abscence of III explains why one set of
paradigms has only a three-way semantic contrast.

Gap for I: Second, we may get a systematic gap for
contrast I. This case frame requires that the verb have an
object in its semantics; consequently, if a verb does not
have an object, we will not be able to create case frame I
by the intransitive rule. This means that such a verb will
have a gap for contrast I, resulting in a paradigm with only
three contrasts, as in (8).

(8) Model   Actual Paradigm

    I [Obj___]   ---

    II [Agt ___]   /dauṛ/ 'run'

    III [Agt Agt ___]   /dauṛ-aa/ 'chase'

    IV [Agt Agt ___]   /dauṛ-vaa/ 'have run'

The lack of an object in the verb semantics of (8) leads to
a gap for contrast I, giving us a paradigm with only a
three-way contrast. Thus, the predictable abscence of
contrast I explains why another set of paradigms has only
three members.

Gaps for both I and III: A paradigm may show gaps for
both I and III. (9) exemplifies a paradigm that lacks
distinction I on phonological grounds because this verb

lacks a long stem vowel required by the intransitive rule; and it lacks distinction III because the Base verb does not have an affected subject. As such, this paradigm ends up with only a two-way semantic contrast.

(9) <u>Model</u>   <u>Actual</u> <u>Paradigm</u>

    I [Obj __]   ---

    II [Agt Obj __]   /kar/ 'do'

    III [Agt Agt Obj __]   ---

    IV [Agt Agt Obj __]   /kar-aa/-/kar-vaa/ 'have done'

Thus, claiming that (9) has gaps for contrasts I and III explains why one set of verbs has only a two-way semantic contrast, despite the four-way contrast available to other verbs.

To conclude, we can systematically predict which contrasts of (1) will be absent and thereby explain why paradigms contain a seemingly erratic number of contrasts. Thus, model (1) renders these differences in the data systematic, making it unnecessary to set up the verb classes earlier grammarians posited to account for these paradigmatic differences. This results in an enormous simplification of the grammar.

A transformational model of Hindi causatives (Kachru 1966, 1971; Kleiman 1971) expresses semantic generalizations in terms of actual derivations; and as a result, it cannot incorporate the notion of semantic gaps. Such an analysis

fails to be explanatory for two reasons. First, one cannot
explain why a semantic generalization associated with a
stage of causation in one set of verbs cannot be associated
with the same stage of causation in another set of verbs.
Second, since this data is not analyzed as involving gaps,
there is no generalization on upper bounds; for now there is
no way of distinguishing between the maximum number of four
contrasts permitted in the language from the maximum number
of (two, three, or four) contrasts permitted to different
verbs.

Thus, the notion of gaps brings system into an area
otherwise rife with confusion; and this notion becomes
possible only if we recognize an abstract model, distinct
from the derivational process, against which semantic
contrasts created by the latter can be classified.

2.3 Systematic Vs. Accidental Semantic Gaps

With the notion of semantic gaps we can create a
further explanatory distinction--that between systematic vs.
accidental semantic gaps.

Systematic semantic gaps result if the semantic
prerequisites for a particular contrast specified by the
model paradigm (1) are not met; semantically accidental gaps
occur when semantic prerequisites are met but the expected
contrast fails to show up, sometimes for phonological or

other reasons, other times for no reason at all.

Gap for I: One semantically accidental gap has already been shown for contrast I in paradigm (9). This gap has a phonological basis since the stem vowel shortening required for contrast I is not possible with the verb /kar/ 'do'.

Similarly, the semantically systematic lack of case frame I in (8) contrasts with the semantically accidental, but phonologically systematic lack of contrast I in (10).

(10) Model   Actual Paradigm

   I [Obj ___]   ?/khay/ 'get eaten'

   II [Agt Obj ___]   /khaa/ 'eat'

   III [Agt Agt Obj ___]   /khil-aa/ 'feed'

   IV [Agt Agt Obj ___]   /khil-vaa/ 'have eat/eaten'

In this paradigm [as also in (11)], application of the intransitive rule could derive I from II; however, the resulting forms */kha/ and */ga/ are phonologically unacceptable because of the final schwa. As a result, these forms exist marginally[1] with the insertion of a final glide.

Gap for III: For contrast III, a semantically systematic gap was presented in (8), where the verb /kaṭ/ did not have an affected subject. This semantically systematic gap contrasts with a semantically accidental, though phonologically systematic gap for III in paradigm (11) because the verb /gaa/ of the latter can (optionally) have an affected subject.

(11) I [Obj __]   ??/gay/ 'sung'

    II [Agt Obj __]   /gaa/ 'sing'

    III [Agt Agt Obj __]   */ga-aa/ 'make sing'

    IV [Agt Agt Obj __]   /ga-vaa/ 'have sing'

Since the subject of /gaa/ can be +affected, this verb meets
the semantic requirements of having both an involved causer
and an affected causee required for III. However, the
resulting form */ga-aa/ would be phonologically unacceptable
because of the vowel sequence. Often such vowel sequences
are   broken   by /l/   insertion (e.g.   /khaa/   'eat'   →
/khil-aa/), but such is not the case here--perhaps because
/l/ insertion in this instance would yield /gal-aa/, a   form
that already exists with the meaning 'tenderize'.

    The distinction between semantically systematic and
semantically accidental gaps is highly explanatory in the
grammar. First, accidental gaps can   show   up   marginally,
e.g., case frame I in paradigms (10) and (11). Second,
these gaps may be absent in one dialect but show up in
another,[2] so that it is doubtful if many of them could be
considered gaps in the collective <u>langue</u>.   Thus,   an
explanatory grammar must be able to distinguish systematic
gaps from accidental gaps, ruling out the former while
potentially allowing the latter. The distinction between
the two types of gaps becomes possible because model (1)

permits only systematically possible verbs.

3. EXPLANATORY VALUE FOR UNIVERSAL GRAMMAR

Model (1) specifies the number and precise type of contrasts paradigms may contain, as well as their prerequisites. As a result, it provides an extremely constrained model of universal causative paradigms.

Section 2.1 showed that this model is able to state the upper bounds in Hindi; and 2.2 showed that using the notion of gaps we can give the same general description to all Hindi paradigms despite their seeming differences.

In a parallel manner, model (1) enables us to state the upper bounds of universal causativization, and to account for paradigmatic differences--across languages, as well as within languages, rendering them systematic and predictable.

3.1 Upper Bounds

Cross-linguistically, languages have very strong constraints on the number of causative contrasts a paradigm may contain, for which no explanation is yet available.

The question of paradigmatic upper bounds has been raised before, in Givon 1976, who (pp 336-339) offers an explanation for Bantu languages in terms of a shortage of c.m. He says these upper bounds are:

probably motivated by speech processing considerations, i.e., the lack of sufficient case markings to differentiate the semantic function of the various object nominals following the verb, since every application of lexical causativization increases the transitivity of the verb by one nominal object... To sum up, then, it seems that the language has established an UPPER BOUND on causativization here, and that a speech processing motivation for this type of constraint is the most likely explanation. It is, thus, a constraint on the complexity of surface structures of causative expressions, motivated by the great difficulty of telling the functions of the various "accusatives" apart.

However, Givon's explanation would not hold true for languages such as Hindi.

Like the Bantu data discussed in Givon (1976), Hindi too has restrictions against multiple instances of the dative-accusative case marking. To illustrate, the causative sentence (12) may mark its causee by either -koo or -see.

(12) mai-nee harkaaree-koo/-see citthii likh-vaa-ii

I-agt scribe-D/A/instr letter write-IC-past

I had the scribe write a letter.

If, however, the sentence were to also contain a dative (which must be marked by -koo), then the causee would obligatorily be marked -see, as in (13).

(13) mai-nee harkaaree-see/*-koo siitaa-koo citthii

likh-vaa-ii

I-agt   scribe-instr/*D/A   Sita-D/A   letter

write-IC-past

I had the scribe write a letter to Sita.

However, this restriction does not prevent Hindi
sentences from having multiple causees marked by the
instrumental c.m., as in (14), where linear order
facilitates interpretation.

> (14) mai-nee   siitaa-see   raam-see   naukar-see   peer
>
>   kaṭ-vaa-yaa
>
>   I-agt   Sita-instr   Ram-instr   servant-instr   tree
>
>   cut-IC-past
>
>   I had   Sita   make   Ram   make   the servant cut the
>
>   tree.

Thus, it is not the lack of a sufficient number of case
markings that prevents causativization from being
morphologically expressed after a fixed a number of stages.
Consequently, an explanation in terms of a shortage of c.m.
is not adequate for universal upper bounds. Model (1), by
contrast, simply does not allow more than four members,
regardless of c.m. availability.

To conclude, causative paradigms never contain more
than four semantically contrastive members. This is a very
strong constraint on universal paradigms, and model (1) is
able to express it in a principled manner.

3.2 Paradigmatic Differences Across Languages

Not all languages permit the four-way contrast claimed by model (1), and attested in languages such as Hindi; this may lead one to think that a four-way model may not be universally appropriate. However, these cross-linguistic differences in the number of contrasts can be systematically accounted for by using the notion of gaps already developed in 2.2. Thus, if some languages do not have a four-way paradigm, it is so because in these languages some of the contrasts of (1) are systematic gaps, predictable from the limitations of their causativising mechanism.

We will demonstrate why some languages will systematically not have verbs for IV; why others will have verbs for III and IV only in complementary distribution; and why still others will not have verbs for I. All of these abscences are systematic gaps created by the limitations of the language-specific derivational mechanism.

Gap for IV: Many languages such as English do not have four-way causative paradigms; more specifically, they lack contrast IV conveying noncontactive causation. Thus, English yields the verbs of (15)-(17), corresponding to I-III of (1), but none corresponding to IV.

(15) The bible reads easily.

(16) John reads/studies the bible.

(17) Mr. Jones taught John the bible.

Armenian, Arabic, and Greek provide other examples which yield contactives, but not noncontactives. Armenian yields contactives with intransitives and some transitives; e.g., /hish/, 'remember' vs. /hishecn/ 'remind', /ut/ 'eat' vs. /utecn/ 'feed'; /kem/ 'drink' vs. /kemecn/ 'give drink to'. Arabic yields contactives from intransitives, e.g., /birik/ 'kneel' vs. /birrik/ 'make s.o. kneel', and some transitives, e.g., /fihim/ 'understand' vs. /fahham/ 'make understand'. Greek verbs can be used transitively or intransitively (similar to English 'walk,intr' vs. 'walk,tr'), and those such as /mathéno/ can be interpreted as either the transitive 'learn' or the double-transitive 'teach'.

Using model (1), the lack of contrast IV in these languages is systematic and predictable. Causatives in the languages noted here do not have a means of signalling a noninvolved causer; moreover, their causative formation is restricted to verbs that yield only +affected causees. Thus, by the definition of contactive causation developed in Chapter VI (and summarized in section 3.1 of this chapter), these languages cannot form noncontactive causatives (Ch. VI.4.1), rendering this frame a systematic, predictable gap.

Gaps for III or IV in Complementary Distribution: These can be found in Bengali and Telegu.

Bengali yields contactives with intransitives, e.g.,

/jal/ 'burn' - /jal-aa/ 'light, kindle' and some
transitives, e.g., /par̥/ 'study' - /par̥-aa/ 'teach' but
noncontactives with other transitives, e.g., /kar/ 'do' -
/kar-aa/ 'have do'. Telegu yields contactives with some
transitives, e.g., /tinu/ 'eat' - /tinipincu/ 'feed', but
noncontactives with other transitives, e.g., /kattu/ 'build'
- /katt-incu/ 'have build'.

Given the definition of contactive causation developed
in Ch. VI, the fact that some verbs systematically lack
contactive causatives while others systematically lack
noncontactive causatives in these languages is to be
expected (Ch. VI.4.1). This means that paradigms in these
languages cannot yield a four-way contrast because either
contrast III or contrast IV is a systematic gap.

Gap for I: If a language does not have a rule of
pseudopassive, intransitive verb formation, a contrast I in
this language will be absent.

Thus, model (1) can not only be applied to languages
that do not have four-way paradigms, but it actually serves
an explanatory function.

2.3 Paradigmatic Differences within Languages

Paradigms within a language too differ in the number of contrasts they contain. Model (1) is able to explain these differences in terms of lexical restrictions that create systematic gaps for contrasts III and I, similar to the ones we saw for Hindi.

Gap for III: In languages such as Hindi that have a two suffix system, suffix A which creates contactive causatives with one set of verbs fails to do so with a second set of verbs, producing instead noncontactives just as suffix B does regularly. This yields a gap for contrast III (together with 'morphological alternates' for IV). This phenomenon was illustrated for Hindi in (4)-(5).

In a parallel manner, the Finnish suffixes TA and TUTTA signal the contrast between contactive and noncontactive causation in paradigms like /kulke/ 'go' /kuljetta/ 'bring' /kuljetutta/ 'bring with someone's help', but fail to signal this contrast with other paradigms like /vetää/ 'pull' vs. /vedättää/ - /vedätyttää/ 'have pull'. In Turkish, iteration of the causative morpheme creates semantic contrast with verbs such as /ol/ 'die' /oldür/ 'kill' /öldürt/ 'have someone killed', but not with others such as /de/ 'say' vs. /de-dir/ - /de-dir-t/ 'have say'. Finally, the Malayalam suffixes create the contactive-noncontactive contrast in paradigms like /ariy/

'know' /ariyikk/ 'make known' /arivippikk/ 'cause to make known', but not in others like /cey/ 'do' vs. /ceyy-ikk/ - /ceyy-ipp-ikk/ 'have do'.

In this way, using model (1), it becomes expected why some paradigms lack a contrast found in other paradigms in the same language, and why this missing frame happens to be a contactive causative.

Gap for I: Even if a language has a mechanism for deriving I, some paradigms will not have this contrast. Such a gap for I can also be explained lexically; for if a verb does not have an object, case frame I is a logical impossibility.

To conclude, universal causative paradigms are not infinitely varied in the number and type of contrasts they display; rather, we see the same patterns repeated. Paradigm (1) captures these recurrent semantic patterns of universal causative paradigms, expressing the very strong constraints of number and type on the contrasts they contain, and rendering their seeming differences systematic and predictable.

3.4 Derivational Problems

The semantic parameters of (1) enable us to express causative relationships where doing so by means of actual derivations would be problematic.

For example, we would like to be able to consider verbs like English 'feed', 'teach', and 'kill' as being in the same paradigm as 'eat', 'read/study', and 'die', respectively. Despite any idiosyncratic information the former may contain, these pairs nevertheless contain much semantic information in common.

The transformational model expresses this relationship by deriving verbs such as 'feed' from a causative embedding of verbs such as 'eat'. However, claiming that such derivations are possible and desirable has been much debated (e.g., Fodor 1970).

However, using model (1) it is possible to declare these verbs as being in the same causative paradigm without making claims of derivability. This is because model (1) permits a Case Grammar type of analysis, where 'feed' can be analyzed as the (A A O _) version of the (A O _) verb 'eat'.

To conclude, causatives frequently acquire idiosyncrasy, which makes claims of derivability controversial. Since model (1) abstracts only the role in verbs entries (rather than involve total verb semantics), it allows us to count certain verbs as being causatives without making claims of derivability.

3.5 Markedness Observations

The semantic generalizations of model (1) permit
interesting observations in terms of universal markedness.

Frame IV, representing noncontactive causation is the
most highly marked case frame. (i) Such causatives are
statistically restricted across languages, e.g., English
does not have them. (ii) In languages that have these
frames, they are almost always morphologically derived
(rather than basic). Thus, (iii) they are almost
exclusively restricted to languages with overt morphological
marking of causatives. Languages such as English that lack
morphologically overt causatives typically rely on ordinary
embedding (e.g., 'I had John cut the cloth') to express the
semantics expressed by these frames. (In 3.2 we observed
that languages that do not have an appropriate suffixal
mechanism will show a gap for this frame.)

Frame III, i.e., contactive causation involving a
causer agent and a causee agent, is much less marked because
the close association between the causer and the causee
provides the basis for binding them in a single activity
where the causer is an agent and the affected causee is the
patient in a quasi-transitive verb.[3] (i) These causatives
are statistically frequent across languages, and (ii) they

can occur as basic words (rather than being morphologically derived from other words), e.g., English 'feed', 'chase', 'teach', etc. Thus, languages do not need an overt morphological system to express these causatives. (iii) Even if a language expresses this semantics by clearly suffixal mechanism, the tendency is for increasing lexicalization. (iv) Because of the markedness difference involved, contactive causatives are introduced in a language before noncontactives, e.g., English has contactives such as 'feed' and 'teach', but not noncontactives such as 'have eat' and 'have study' (as single words). Consequently, (iv) we can expect that if a language has noncontactive causatives, it will also have contactive causatives. (We observed in sections 3.2 and 3.3 that gaps for this frame occur not because of the limitations of causativizing mechanism, but only because of lexical limitations, i.e., the Base verb does not have an affected subject.)

Frame II--contactive causation involving a causer and a patient--semantically a simple transitive verb, is the basic, unmarked frame. Why this should be less marked than the (other) causative frames is understandable: we expect agents to typically affect inanimate objects rather than other agents who have their own volition and energy. Thus, (i) this frame can be found in every language, i.e., is never a gap in any language. (ii) In any given language, this is the most frequent frame of all. (iii) It is typically basic rather than derived, as in Hindi (Ch. II). As a corollary, (iv) overwhelmingly, this frame is morphologically unmarked.

The frame (O_) is also a marked frame. This is to be expected because (as explained in Ch. II) in the world of humans, human intervention becomes important and therefore highly frequent in linguistic encoding. As such, except for a limited number of events involving natural phenomena (e.g., 'The door opened'), objects are typically conceptualized as undergoing change of state at the hands of an agent, rather than by themselves. Thus, the conceptualization of agent-motivated activity in an (O_) frame is a marked situation. As such, (i) this frame is infrequent in languages of the world; for example, English has only a handful of 'pseudopassive' intransitive verbs representing agent-motivated activity--as in 'The book reads easily'. (ii) Such verbs are syntactically marked; for example, English expressions such as 'The book reads easily' require an obligatory adverb. (iii) Such verbs are typically derived (rather than basic); e.g., as shown in Chapter II, Hindi provides clear evidence that (O_) verbs representing agent-motivated activity are derived from (AO_) verbs. (We saw in section 3. that gaps for this frame occur if either the language does not have a rule of pseudopassive, intransitive formation, or because of lexical limitations--i.e., the verb lacks a patient role in its semantics.)

4. CONCLUSION

To conclude, the four significant semantic generalizations of causative paradigms cannot be expressed in terms of the popular, derivational notions of (First/Second) causative vs. noncausative, and must be abstracted into a formal model, (1).

Recognizing such a model has much explanatory value. This model captures the universally recurring semantic patterns of paradigm contrasts in a highly constrained manner, stating both their number and the precise types that are permitted. It enables us to give the same uniform description to causative paradigms universally, rendering their differences systematic and predictable, and bringing generalizability and constraint into an area that had hitherto not seemed to lend itself to any. Thus, the proposed model is essential if our descriptions of causatives are to gain explanatory adequacy.

NOTES

[1]For me, these verbs are best restricted to the past and are even better with the auxiliary verb /gayaa/, as in sentences (i) and (ii).

(i) saaree paraathee khay gayee

   All the parathas got eaten.

(ii) meeraa vaalaa gaanaa too gay gayaa

   The song (of my choice) has been sung.

[2]For example, discussing one group of verbs, Masica (1976:45) notices that the -aa form is "rare or missing", and that it is "hard to be sure of this as it often occurs dialectally or colloquially somewhere". To give an illustration, two of the four gaps he mentions, viz., /bik-aa/ 'have sell' (p. 44) and /phaṛ-aa/ 'have tear' (p. 45) exist in my personal usage, but the form /mar-aa/ 'have kill' that he presents (p. 44) does not.

In such -aa vs. -vaa 'mergers', the reason why the -aa form is shaky and the -vaa preferred is because the -aa form elsewhere signals contactive causation, whereas the -vaa forms are always associated with noncontactive causation. Thus, given a choice, the latter would be preferred for expressing noncontactive causation.

[3]The relative ease with which contactive causation can be conceptualized is evidenced in two other phenomena. For example, Chapter IV.7 showed that lexicalization, or the addition of idiosyncratic material appears most commonly in contactive causatives (i.e., -aa causatives with -koo or -0 causees). Thus, the contactive causative /ghaṭ-aa/ 'subtract' cannot be completely described as 'cause to become less'; however, the noncontactive /kaṭ-aa/ can be completely described as 'have cut, cause to cut'.

Similarly, the contactive but not noncontactive activity can be viewed from the perspective of causee initiative in a noncausative sentence.

   (iii) maasṭar-nee raam-koo paṛh-aa-yaa

        teacher-agt Ram-D/A study-DC-past

        The teacher taught Ram.

   (iv) maasṭar-nee raam-koo paṛh-vaa-yaa

        teacher-agt Ram-D/A study-IC-past

        The teacher had Ram study.

    (v) raam-nee maasṭar-see paṛh-aa

        Ram-agt teacher-instr study-past

        Ram took instruction from the teacher.

The contactive causative (iii) but not the noncontactive causative (iv) finds semantic equivalence in a noncausative sentence such as (v).

8

LEXICALIZATION*

Thus far, we have focused on the productivity and regularity of Hindi causatives, viz., that the suffixes -aa and -vaa signifying causer involvement vs. noninvolvement can be attached to almost all verbs, and (depending upon the +/-affected property of noncausative agents) signal contactive or noncontactive causation in a predictable manner.

This chapter shows that even such a highly regular and productive system develops idiosyncrasies at all levels--lexical, syntactic, and morphological; as such, idiosyncrasy must be considered integral to causatives, and a separation of causatives into 'lexical' vs. 'productive' (Shibatani 1975) may not be meaningful.

Second, these irregularities also provide a strong empirical argument against a transformational analysis (Kachru 1966, 1971; Kleiman 1971), which would derive Tr verbs from a causative embedding of the corresponding Intr verbs, DC's from a causative embedding of the corresponding Base, and IC's from a causative embedding of the corresponding DC's.

1. SYNTACTIC IDIOSYNCRASY

Gaps: (1) illustrates some gaps in the causative paradigm.

(1)

Base	DC	IC	Gloss
gaa	*ga-aa	ga-vaa	sing
khariid	*kharid-aa	kharid-vaa	buy
lee	*li-aa	li-vaa	take

These gaps are problematic in the transformational derivation of the paradigm. First, T-causative must be prevented from applying to the Base form to yield a DC form. Second, for these paradigms, a DC form is not available from which to derive the corresponding IC form.

(2) presents some gaps in the IC column.

(2)

Verb	Gloss
*kam-vaa	earn-IC
*sadh-vaa	balance-IC
*pahcaan-vaa	recognize-IC
*har-vaa	lose-IC
*padhaar-vaa	enter welcomed-IC
*cãũk-vaa	surprise-IC
*hãs-vaa	laugh-IC

Thus, the causative transformation must be prevented from yielding the IC forms of (2).

Sentential Gaps: Even when the noncausative verb is
available   for   deriving   a   causative,   the   required
noncausative sentence can be ungrammatical. Thus, although
one can derive (3) from (4), one cannot similarly derive (5)
from (6).

  (3) mai-nee raam-koo chip-aa-yaa

    I-agt Ram-D/A hide-DC-past,m

    I hid Ram.

  (4) raam chip-aa

    Ram hide-past,m

    Ram hid.

  (5) mai-nee saamaan-koo chip-aa-yaa

    I-agt luggage hide-DC-past,m

    I hid the luggage.

  (6)??saamaan chip-aa

    luggage hide-past,m

    The luggage hid.

Another such causative verb is /sambhaal/ 'take care,
balance'.

Nonpredictable Selectional Restrictions: Often, the
selectional   restrictions   of   number   and   animacy   on   a
causative cannot be predicted from those of the
corresponding noncausative. Thus, the noncausative verb
/mil/ may have either a singular or a plural subject, as
shown in (7) and (8).

(7) raam aur siitaa mil-ee

Ram and Sita meet-past,m pl

Ram and Sita met.

(8) (siitaa-koo) raam mil-aa

(Sita-D/A) Ram meet-past,m

Ram was found (by Sita).

However, its causatives require their objects to be plural.

(9) mai-nee raam aur siitaa-koo mil-aa-yaa

I-agt Ram and Sita D/A meet-DC-past,m

I made Ram and Sita meet.

(10)*mai-nee (siitaa-koo) raam mil-aa-yaa

(11)*mai-nee (siitaa-koo) raam mil-vaa-yaa

Similar restrictions may exist for animacy. Thus, the subject of the Intr /mur̥/ may be either inanimate or animate.

(12) kaagaz mur̥-aa

paper turn-past,m

The paper folded.

(13) raam mur̥-aa

Ram turn-past,m

Ram turned.

However, its Tr, DC, and IC require that their objects be inanimate.

(14) mai-nee kaagaz-koo moor̥-aa

I-agt paper-D/A turn-past,m

I folded the paper.

(15)*mai-nee raam-koo moor-aa

(16)*mai-nee raam-koo mur-aa-yaa /mur-vaa-yaa

The verb <u>badal</u> is parallel.

(17) kapraa badl-aa

cloth change-past,m

The cloth (was) changed.

(18) raam badl-aa

Ram change-past

Ram changed.

(19) mai-nee kapree-koo badal-vaa-yaa

I-agt cloth-D/A change-IC-past,m

I had the cloth changed.

(20)*mai-nee raam-koo badal-vaa-yaa

I-agt Ram-D/A change-IC-past,m

I had Ram change.

So is the verb /camak/.

(21) bartan camk-aa

utensil shine-past,m

The utensil shone.

(22) raam camk-aa

Ram shine-past,m

Ram shone (= stood out).

(23) mai-nee bartan-koo camk-aa-yaa/camak-vaa-yaa

I-agt dish-D/A shine-DC-past,m/shine-IC-past,m

I made/had the utensil shine.

(24)*mai-nee raam-koo camk-aa-yaa/camak-vaa-yaa

I-agt Ram-D/A shine-DC-past,m/shine-IC-past,m

I made/had Ram stand out.

The above examples show that the object of the causative cannot always be equated with the subject of the noncausative.

Non-unique Causative Relations: Many noncausative verbs must be related to more than one DC or IC, and these are often in unpredictable complementary distribution, as in (25)-(27).

(25) raam ḍuub-aa

ram drown-past

Ram drowned.

(26) siitaa-nee raam-koo gangaajii-mee ḍub-aa-yaa

Sita-agt Ram-D/A Ganges-in drown-DC-past

Sita drowned Ram in the Ganges.

(27) siitaa-nee raam-koo gangaajii-mee dub-oo-yaa

*Sita drowned Ram in the Ganges.

Sita dipped Ram in the Ganges.

The grammatical reading of (27) is facilitated by assuming that Ram was a baby or an invalid.

Idiosyncratic Functional Roles: Often, the functional roles of a causative verb cannot be predicted from those of the noncausative. Thus:

(28)   luṭ   luuṭ   luṭ-aa

       O__   AO__   AO__

                                          *AA__

    O PLUNDERED   A PLUNDERS O   A GIVES AWAY O

                                        *A MAKES A PLUNDER O

2. SEMANTIC IDIOSYNCRASY

Try-Cause: Causative   verbs   normally   have   the semantics (29).

(29)   AGENT CAUSES [Base Semantics]

However,   many   causatives   idiosyncratically   acquire   the semantic feature TRY, yielding the semantics (30).

(30)   AGENT TRIES TO CAUSE   [Base Semantics]

As a consequence, (31) is legitimate.

(31) mai-nee raam-koo haṭ-aa/vaa-yaa   par   voh   nahĩĩ
         haṭ-aa

      I-agt Ram-D/A move-DC/IC-past,m   but   he   not

      move-past,m

      I tried to (have) Ram move, but he didn't move.

In   the   T-framework,   the   underlying   structure   of   (31) represents   a   contradiction,   and   the   sentence   should   be anomalous.

Notice that the   feature   TRY   cannot   be   linked   with T-cause   because   most   causatives   do not permit it.   Thus, (32) is anomalous.

(32)*mai-nee raam-see peeṛ kaṭ-aa-yaa par us-nee

nahĩ̃ kaaṭ-aa

I-agt Ram-instr tree cut-DC-past,m but he-agt not

cut-past,m

I had Ram cut the tree, but he didn't cut it.

<u>Arbitrarily</u> <u>Restricted</u> <u>Semantics</u>: Often, only arbi-

trarily chosen meanings of a verb causativize. Thus:

(33) | <u>V</u> | <u>V-DC</u> | <u>V-IC</u> |
|---|---|---|
| pak | pak-aa | pak-vaa |
| GET COOKED | COOK | HAVE O COOKED |
| GET RIPE | *RIPEN | *HAVE O RIPENED |

(34) | <u>V</u> | <u>V-DC</u> | <u>V-IC</u> |
|---|---|---|
| bac | bac-aa | bac-vaa |
| O IS SAVED | A SAVES O | A HAS O SAVED |
| A IS CAREFUL | *A MAKES A CAREFUL | *A HAS A BE CAREFUL |

<u>Idiosyncratic</u> <u>derivation</u>: When either the Intr or DC

contains idiosyncratic information, it is unpredictable

whether the IC will be based on the Intr, the Base, or the

DC. Thus, although the IC semantics is predictable from one

of these forms, there is no automatic procedure for deciding

which form to take as basic. That is to say, reference to a
specific base form needs to be specified individually for
each of these IC's. For example, the IC of (35) is related
to the Intr but not to the Tr/Base form.

(35)   Intr   Tr/Base   IC

       ḍaṭ   ḍaaṭ   ḍaṭ-vaa
       be spruce   scold   have (s.o.) be spruce
                                            *have (s.o.) scold

       mar   maar   mar-vaa
       die   hit   have (s.o.) killed
                                            *have (s.o.) hit

In (36) the IC must refer to the DC form, not the Base form.

(36)   Base   DC   IC

       pak   pak-aa   pak-vaa
       cook, ripen   cook (something)   have (stg) cook
                       *ripen (stg)   *have (stg) ripened

       bool   bul-aa   bul-vaa
       speak   call (s.o.)   have (s.o.) called
                       *make (A) speak   *have (A) speak

       luuṭ   luṭ-aa   luṭ-vaa
       plunder   give away   have (A) give away
                       *make (A) plunder   *have (A) plunder

Semantic Opaqueness: Often, the causative reading
cannot be rendered very literally. Thus:

   (37) phuul carh-aa-naa

        flowers ascend-DC-inf

        offer, shower flowers in the temple

        ≠ CAUSE FLOWERS TO ASCEND

   (38) baccaa khil-aa-naa

        child play-DC-inf

take care of a child

≠ CAUSE THE CHILD TO PLAY

(39) thahr-aa-naa
.

wait-DC-inf

provide temporary lodgings

≠CAUSE TO WAIT

(40) ghat-aa-naa
.

become less-DC-inf

subtract

≠ CAUSE TO BECOME LESS

(41) pakr-aa-naa
.

hold-DC-inf

hand (stg)

?= CAUSE TO HOLD

(42) sun-aa-naa

listen-DC-inf

narrate

≠ CAUSE TO LISTEN

Irregular semantics: There are many causatives whose
semantics cannot be predicted from any of the other forms in
the paradigm.

(43) Base   DC   IC

      mããg   mãg-aa   mãg-vaa
      ask   send for   order (= purchase)

      kah   kah-laa   kahal-vaa
      say   send word   have (stg) said to (s.o.)

      bool   bul-aa   bul-vaa

speak   call, invite   have called

paṭ   paṭ-aa   paṭ-vaa
get along   talk (s.o.) into   lay floor, roof

cuuk   cuk-aa   cuk-vaa
miss   pay up   have pay up

lee   --   li-vaa
take   buy (stg) for (s.o.)

3. MORPHOLOGICAL IDIOSYNCRASY

Split Paradigms: When a noncausative has two DC's,
it is unpredictable whether there will be an IC
corresponding to each, or whether there will be only one IC
for both DC's. Furthermore, if there is only a single IC,
we do not know to which DC it will correspond.

(44) Base   DC   IC   Gloss

      ḍuub   ḍub-aa   ḍub-vaa   drown
                ḍub-oo

      kah   kah-laa   kah-vaa   say
                kah-laa   kahal-vaa

      siikh   sikh-aa   sikh-vaa   learn
                sikh-laa   *sikhal-vaa

The IC may itself split the paradigm by producing two
alternating forms.

(45) Base   DC   IC   Gloss

      beec   bik-aa   bik-vaa   sell
                            bic-vaa

      khaa   khil-aa   khil-vaa   eat
                            kha-vaa

Subregularities: Some causatives are exceptions to the general morpho-phonological rules of causative formation. However, these exceptions constitute minor regularities for a handful of items. For example, a DC is normally expressed by the suffix -aa; with some verbs, however, this suffix may be realized as -oo.

(46)

Base	DC	Gloss
ḍuub	ḍub-aa/ḍub-oo	drown
bhiig	bhig-aa/bhig-oo	wet

Another minor causative rule is illustrated by the causative alternation in (47).

(47)

Intr	Base	Gloss
chuuṭ	choor̤	free
tuuṭ	toor̤	break
phuuṭ	phoor̤	split
phaṭ	phaar̤	tear

Total idiosyncrasy: Even after the above subregularities have been noted, we still find examples of total idiosyncrasy. For example, a general morphological process shortens long stem vowels before long vowel suffixes. This process shortens /ee/ and /ii/ to /i/, and /oo/ and /uu/ to /u/ before the causative suffixes -aa and -vaa. Idiosyncratically, however, we find instances of /ai/ → /i/ and /aa/ → to /i/.

(48)   baiṭh   biṭh-aa   sit

        khaa   khil-aa   eat

Finally, (49) provides examples of assorted irregularities.

(49)   <u>Verb</u>   <u>Causative</u>   <u>Gloss</u>

        bik   beec   sell

        kah   kah-laa   say

        jaan   jat-laa   know

        baiṭh   baiṭh-(l)aa, biṭh-(l)aa   sit

                     baiṭh-aal, biṭh-aal

<u>Cross-classification</u> <u>of</u> <u>morphology</u> <u>and</u> <u>syntax</u>:   Some
causatives have a semantic alternation but no corresponding
morphological alternation.

    (50) saamaan badl-aa

         luggage change-past,m

         The luggage (was) changed.

    (51) mai-nee saamaan badl-aa

         I-agt luggage change-past,m

         I changed the luggage.

    Conversely, some causatives have a morphological
causative alternation but no semantic alternation.   Thus,
/bhag, bhaag/ 'run away'; /chuṭ, chuuṭ/ 'get removed'; /jag,
jaag/ 'wake up'.

    Finally, there are verbs which are morphologically but
not semantically in a causative relationship.

(52)   mar 'die'   maar 'hit'

har 'pillage'   haar 'lose'

gar 'prick (stg)'   gaar 'plant (stg)'

The   above data indicate that causative morphology and
syntax do not always synchronize. A transformation predicts
morphology, semantics, and syntax simultaneously; as such, a
causative transformation is not appropriate for these data.

To   conclude, this   chapter has provided an empirical
basis for   resolving   the   lexicalist vs.   transformational
controversy.   The   variety   and   extent   of   causative
irregularity   destroys   fundamental   claims   that   give
transformations   their   explanatory   power.   Transformations
are productive, but causative paradigms have numerous gaps;
transformations   apply with blind regularity, but causatives
are exception-ridden; transformations preserve meaning, but
causativization   does not. Thus, transformations are not an
appropriate   mechanism   for   the   derivation   of   Hindi
causatives.

NOTE

*An   earlier   version of this chapter was presented at
the 1974 LSA   Winter   Meeting   as   "Causative   Idiosyncrasy:
Argument for a Lexicalist Analysis".

9

A FORMAL MODEL FOR LEXICAL ENTRIES

We now have many types of arguments against a transformational analysis of Hindi causatives. Chapter II argued that Tr cannot be derived from Intr (by a causative transformation), Chapter III argued against introducing the causative agent (by a causative transformation), and Chapter VIII provided the idiosyncrasy argument against this analysis. These conclusions are further supported by the findings of Saksena (1975b), which shows that a constraint involving the case marking -koo treats causatives as simplexes.[1]

Since causatives are characterized by generalizations as well as idiosyncrasy, an adequate model must be able to express both these aspects of the data. A model capable of doing so has been proposed by Jackendoff (1975) to account for morphological and semantic regularities in the lexicon for English, and it can easily be modified for Hindi.

Essentially, this model recognizes a set of lexical redundancy rules for stating lexical generalizations, as well as a lexicon with fully specified verb entries. Thus,

the   lexicon   contains both causative and noncausative verbs
and their entries contain both predictable and idiosyncratic
information.   Because   entries   are   listed   in their fully
specified form, the redundancy rules play   no   part   in   the
derivation of these entries, only in their evaluation.   They
do so by specifying a portion of these verb   entries   to   be
predictable,   and   by   assigning   cost   to   the   remaining,
nonpredictable information.   Since cost is not   assigned   to
the   predictable   portion   of verb entries, this practice of
listing   fully   specified   entries   is   without   harm.   For
further   details   on   this   model, the reader is referred to
Jackendoff (1975).

1. RULES

1.1 Hindi-Specific Rules

Three   Hindi-specific   redundancy   rules   for   the
morpho-semanto-syntactic generalizations in Hindi   paradigms
have   been   motivated   in   earlier   chapters;   these   can be
schematized as in (1).[2]

(1)

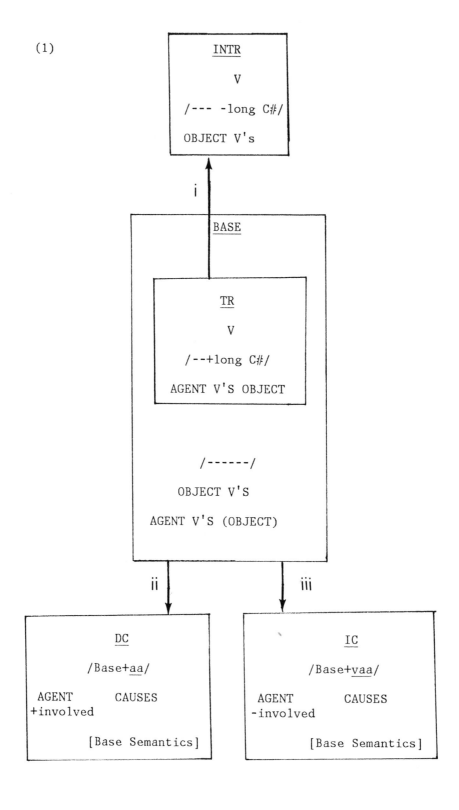

Rule (i) says that if a Base verb has a long stem
vowel and transitive syntax, then we can get a corresponding
intransitive with a short stem vowel (Chapter II).

Rule (ii) says that Base verbs may take a suffix -aa,
and the resulting DC form is a causative with a personally
involved causer (Chapter VI).

Rule (iii) says that Base verbs may take a suffix
-vaa, and the resulting IC form is a causative with a
noninvolved causer (Chapter VI).

1.2 Language-General Rules

In addition to the three Hindi-specific rules of verb
formation, we have two language-general rules for specifying
the semantics of contact (as discussed in Chapter VI).

$$(iv) \begin{bmatrix} \text{AGENT} & \text{CAUSES} \\ \text{+involved} \\ \\ & [\text{NP V (NP)}] \\ & \text{+aff} \end{bmatrix} \longrightarrow \begin{bmatrix} \text{+CAUSATIVE} \\ \text{+CONTACTIVE} \end{bmatrix}$$

where NP $\longrightarrow$ patient, dative, experiencer, aff agent
+aff

Rule (iv) says that a causative verb with an involved causer
and an affected causee is redundantly a contactive
causative; furthermore, patients, experiencers, datives, and
affected agents count as affected NP's.

(v) $\begin{bmatrix} \text{AGENT} \quad \text{CAUSES} \\ \text{-involved} \\ \\ \quad\quad [\text{NP V NP}] \\ \quad\quad \text{-aff} \end{bmatrix} \longrightarrow \begin{bmatrix} +\text{CAUSATIVE} \\ -\text{CONTACTIVE} \end{bmatrix}$

Rule (v) says that a causative verb with either a noninvolved causer or a nonaffected causee is redundantly a noncontactive causative.

2. PREDICTABILITY IN VERB ENTRIES

The rules given above can be exemplified by entries for sample paradigms.

2.1 Example One

Paradigm (2) provides an example of how regularities are captured by Redundancy Rules (i)-(v).

(2) Intr   Tr / Base

/dikh/   /deekh/

OBJECT (GETS) SEEN   AGENT SEES OBJECT
                             +aff

DC   IC

/dikh-aa/   /dikh-vaa/

AGENT CAUSES   AGENT CAUSES
+involved   -involved

   [AGENT SEE OBJECT]   [AGENT SEE OBJECT]
   +aff   +aff

In (2), the Base verb /deekh/ 'look, see' has a long stem
vowel and transitive syntax; consequently, the corresponding
Intr verb /dikh/ '(get) seen', which has a short stem vowel
and intransitive syntax, is predictable by Rule (i). The DC
form /dikh-aa/ 'show', which has an involved causer, is
predictable by Rule (ii) and the IC form /dikh-vaa/ 'have
see', which has a noninvolved causer, is predictable by Rule
(iii).

Since the DC /dikh-aa/ has an involved causer and an
affected   causee,   it signals contactive causation, as
predicted by Rule (iv); and since the IC form /dikh-vaa/ has
a noninvolved causer, it signals noncontactive causation, as
predicted by Rule (v).

2.2 Example Two

Paradigm (3) provides a second example of how
regularities are captured by Redundancy Rules (i)-(v).

(3) <u>Base</u>   <u>DC</u>   <u>IC</u>

/ban/   /ban-aa/   /ban-vaa/

OBJECT MADE   AGENT CAUSES   AGENT CAUSES
+involved   -involved

[OBJECT MADE]   [OBJECT MADE]

In (3), the Base verb has neither a long stem vowel nor
transitive syntax: consequently, Rule (i) is not relevant.
However, as predicted by Rule (ii), we get a DC form
/ban-aa/, with an involved causer, and an IC form /ban-vaa/

with a noninvolved causer.

Since the DC form /ban-aa/ has an involved causer and
a patient (i.e., affected) causee, it signals contactive
causation, as predicted by Rule (iv); and since the IC form
/ban-vaa/ has a noninvolved causer, it signals noncontactive
causation, as predicted by Rule (v).

2.3 Example Three

(4) provides a third example of how the redundancy
rules work.

(4) Base   DC   IC

     /kar/   /kar-aa/   /kar-vaa/

     AGENT DO OBJ   AGENT CAUSES   AGENT CAUSES
     -aff   -involved   -involved

                     [AGENT DO OBJECT] [AGENT DO OBJECT]
                     -aff   -aff

In (4), although the Base verb /kar/ 'do' has transitive
syntax, it does not have a long stem vowel, so that Rule (i)
cannot apply.   However, the DC form /kar-aa/, with an
involved causer, is predictable by Rule (ii), and the IC
form /kar-vaa/, with a noninvolved causer, is predictable by
Rule (iii). Since the DC form /kar-aa/ has a nonaffected
agent, the prerequisite of an affected causee for Rule (iv)
is not met; instead, this form qualifies for Rule (v) and
therefore signals noncontactive causation.   The form
/kar-vaa/ with both a noninvolved causer and a nonaffected

causee also qualifies for Rule (v)   and   therefore   signals
noncontactive causation.   Thus,   the   forms   /kar-aa/   and
/kar-vaa/ both signal noncontactive causation and differ
only with respect to causer involvement.

3. IDIOSYNCRATIC MATERIAL

Idiosyncratic verb entries need additional information
as well as restrictions which do not follow from Rules
(i)-(v).

3.1 Example One

Consider paradigm (5), discussed in Chapter VIII,
sentences (17)-(20).

(5) **Base**   **DC**   **IC**

/badal/   /badl-aa/   /badal-vaa/

$\begin{Bmatrix} \text{OBJECT} \\ \text{AGENT} \end{Bmatrix}$ CHANGE   AGENT CAUSES   AGENT CAUSES
+aff   +involved   -involved
                      -aff   -aff

                  $\begin{Bmatrix} \text{[OBJECT]} \\ \text{*AGENT} \end{Bmatrix}$ CHANGE] $\begin{Bmatrix} \text{[OBJECT]} \\ \text{*AGENT} \end{Bmatrix}$ CHANGE]
                  +aff   +aff

Rule (i) is not applicable to paradigm (5), but Rules (ii)
and (iii) yield the DC and the IC forms with involved and
noninvolved causers, respectively.

Because the DC form contains an involved causer and an
affected causee, it signals contactive causation, as
predicted by Rule (iv); and because the IC form contains a

noninvolved causer, it signals noncontactive causation, as predicted by Rule (v). These aspects of paradigm (5) are completely predictable by Rules (i)-(v), and hence the evaluation metric does not assign cost to them.

However, the paradigm also contains idiosyncratic information: for example, there is no explanation of why the DC and the IC forms are ungrammatical with an agent causee. Consequently, the evaluation metric assigns cost to this portion of the DC and the IC entries.

3.2 Example Two

The entries in (6) show the paradigm discussed in Chapter VIII, example (33).

(6) Base   DC   IC

   /pak/   /pak-aa/   /pak-vaa/

   OBJECT {COOK   AGENT CAUSES   AGENT CAUSES
          {RIPEN   +involved   -involved

                     [OBJECT COOK]   [OBJECT COOK]
                          *RIPEN   *RIPEN

The Base verb of paradigm (6) does not meet the conditions for Rule (i), but Rules (ii) and (iii) yield DC and IC forms with involved vs. noninvolved causers, and Rules (iv) and (v) specify that these forms signal contactive and noncontactive causation, respectively. As such, these aspects of the entries in (6) are not assigned cost. However, the restriction in the DC and the IC entries on the semantics *RIPEN is   arbitrary   and   is   therefore   assigned

cost.

The examples given above illustrate how the lexicalist

model   adopted   here   is   able   to   assign   cost only to the

nonpredictable information in derived   entries.   Thus,   the

greater   the   amount   of   idiosyncratic   information in verb

entries, the greater will be the cost assigned   to   it.   In

this   way, the cost is in direct proportion to the extent of

idiosyncratic information an entry   contains--as   it   should

be.

To conclude: the lexicalist   model   adopted   here   is

simultaneously able to incorporate the idiosyncratic and the

productive aspects of causatives characteristic of the Hindi

data.

NOTES

[1]Balachandran 1973 (originally 1970) argued that participial modifiers, reflexives, and negatives also treat causatives as simplexes, but these claims have been disputed in Kachru 1971, Kleiman 1971.

[2]To prevent overcrowding, the detail concerning optional -see agents in Intr and Base entries, as well as indication of the subject by underlining (as discussed in Chapter III) has been omitted from the entries for sample paradigms in this chapter. However, adding these details poses no technical problems.

Appendix

Shibatani on Lexical vs. Productive Causatives

Shibatani (1975) has proposed a lexical vs. productive distinction in causatives. This apendix argues that such a distinction is neither necessary nor desirable for the description of causatives.

1. ARE THE CONSTRUCTS NECESSARY?

Shibatani presents morphological, syntactic, and semantic criteria for a lexical vs. productive dichotomy. Morphologically, causatives such as Eng. kill are idiosyncratic and restricted, whereas those such as cause to die are regular and productive. Syntactically, the former function as simplexes, the latter as complexes. (Shibatani also considered four semantic criteria, but these do not coincide either with each other or with the syntactically defined classification; as such, they cannot be considered as arguments.)

Shibatani uses Japanese and English as the major languages to argue for the lexical vs. productive contrast. However, the morphological and syntactic differences Shibatani notes in these languages are morphologically overt, and lend themselves to a simple morpheme and word analysis; moreover, such an analysis even explains why the facts noted by Shibatani should hold.

For example, in English, both the morphological and the syntactic facts are exactly what we would expect because these causatives involve a single vs. complex verb/sentence. Thus a lexical vs. productive causative contrast does not shed any additional light on this data.

In Japanese, the morphological differences of idiosyncrasy vs. regularity follow if /sase/ and /as/ are analyzed as regular vs. irregular suffixes; and the syntactic fact that causatives with the latter suffix behave as simplexes follows because these causatives are single-word verbs. The fact that does not follow automatically from a simple morpheme and word analysis is why causatives involving /sase/ (which is presented as a suffix rather than an independent verb) should behave like complexes. However, this data does not involve an issue specific to causatives; rather it addresses the issue of abstractness, viz., whether a surface suffix /sase/ should at some level be analyzed as a separate verb. In this context, however, it would have been interesting to look at the arguments that motivate its analysis as a suffix, as presented.

2. ARE THE NOTIONS ALWAYS WELL DISTINGUISHED?

Having justified the notions lexical and productive
for Japanese and English, Shibatani goes to apply this
distinction to other languages such as Hindi, Quechua, and
Turkish; however, the terms do not carry over well.

2.1 Distinction not Supported

For example, Shibatani professes that Hindi First
causatives are "predominantly lexical" while Second
causatives, are 'productive'.

Morphologically, both the First and Second causative
suffixes -aa and -vaa apply to (almost) all verbs and
equally consistently carry the semantics of causer
involvement vs. noninvolvement (as shown in Chapter VI of
the present work). Syntactically, as Shibatani himself
notes (p 32) "Investigation based on adverbial modification
do not present a particularly clear picture. To a large
extent, phenomena of adverbial modification depend on
adverbs"--i.e., the individual adverb chosen; (p. 33) "Even
with grammatical causative forms, the phenomena of adverbial
modification are not straight-foward", and (p 34) "The
phenomena of adverbial modification in Hindi ... show that
the lexical causatives in this language sometimes behave
like the corresponding English lexical causatives and
sometimes like corresponding English productive causatives".

Thus, there is no basis for separating the -aa from the -vaa causatives, either on morphological or syntactic grounds. As such, the notions lexical and productive are not even clearly defined, much less significant.

2.2 Additional Claim not Supported

Shibatani goes on to assert that First causatives are lexical without productive counterparts, and Second causatives productive without lexical counterparts, making Hindi (along with Quechua, Turkish etc.) a language that does not have (p. 68) "systematic pairs of lexical and productive causative forms"; rather, these languages have "predominantly one form". Given the obvious asymmetry, one wonders how Shibatani arrived at this conclusion.

Shibatani reasons that First causatives signal single causation, Second causatives double causation. However, he does not explain why this property prevents these causatives from pairing as lexical vs. productive counterparts, since the definitions of the terms 'lexical' and 'productive' make no mention of single vs. double causation.

In any event, -vaa causatives are clearly not 'double' causatives (as shown in Ch. VI of the present work), so even Shibatani's reasoning cannot be applied, and the basis for the ensuing generalizations involving "languages with predominantly one form" (p. 39) are rendered questionable.

3. IS THE DISTINCTION DESIRABLE?

It is questionable whether the notions of lexical vs.
productive causatives which link the morpholgical claims of
idiosyncrasy and restriction vs. regularity and productivity
with the syntactic claims of simplexes vs. complexes are, in
fact, desirable.   In Japanese, these morphological and
syntactic claims happen to coincide. However, there is no
principled basis why this correlation should hold, and in
fact, it usually does not.

For example, the Hindi suffixes -aa and -vaa are
productive in the normal linguistic sense: they apply to
almost all verbs, and always, without fail, carry the
semantics of causer involvement vs. noninvolvement; yet,
these suffixes do not behave like complexes in any
systematic manner.

Thus, the morphological claims of idiosyncrasy and
restriction vs. regularity and productivity do not
necessarily correlate with the syntactic claims of simplexes
vs. complexes, and there is no reason why they should.   As
such, the two sets of claims must be separated, not confused
into a single "lexical" vs. "productive" distinction.

4. IS THE DISTINCTION EXPLANATORY?

This can be determined by evaluating the explanations offered.

4.1 Single vs. Multiple Event

One explanation involves the notion of single vs. multiple event. Shibatani claims (p 69) that causatives represent single events when the causee is a patient role, multiple events when the causee is an agent role.

First, Shibatani does not tell us what definitions of the terms agent and patient should be used, making verification difficult beyond the given examples.

Second, the examples given make clear that these notions are used arbitrarily. For example, on p. 70 Shibatani asserts that the Hindi verb 'teach' (which should be padh-aa, not padh) has a patient causee but the verb daur-aa-naa 'make run' has an agent causee. This distinction is a puzzle, since (by the many criteria discussed in Chapters IV-V of the present work) the causees of both verbs equally qualify as (affected) agents (in Hindi as well as English).

Third, what is more, the claims do not hold true even for Shibatani's chosen examples. For example, Shibatani claims (p. 71) that English does not have lexical causative forms for situations in which someone is making someone sing,   dance,   run   etc.   Sentences   such   as 'I danced her around   the   room'   and   'I   ran/chased   him   out'   present counterexamples to this claim.

4.2 Predicting Simplex vs. Complex

Shibatani   makes   two   major   explanations   involving languages such as Hindi, Quechua,   and   Turkish   which   have "predominantly   one   causative   form".   (i) (p. 69) Lexical causatives in such languages behave like simplexes when they denote   a single event and like complexes when they denote a multiple event, and (ii) (p. 69) causatives represent single events   when   the   causee is a patient role, multiple events when the causee is an agent role.

Earlier   it   had   been   stressed   (p.   34)   that   (in languages like Hindi) (iii) whether causatives   behave   like simplexes   or   complexes   depends upon the particular adverb chosen.   The three claims   together   yield   two   inferences: (iv) adverbs determine whether causatives denote a single or multiple event, and (v), adverbs also determine whether   the causee wil be agent or patient.

It is doubtful   whether   Shibatani   actually   intended this inferred information.

5. OTHER PROBLEMS

5.1 Data

The Hindi data reported in Shibatani 1975 is often inaccurate and/or misleading. Thus, on p. 34 example (60), a sentence using the Hindi First causative _sulayaa_ 'make sleep' is included in the discussion of Second causatives: If this inclusion is intentional, what criterion has been used for this grouping?

On several occasions (e.g., p. 70), we come across the verb "_padh-naa_ 'teach'" in which the cited noncausative form does not match the causative gloss; if Shibatani intends the former, the English gloss is a noncausative, viz., 'read, study', but if he intends the latter, the Hindi form is a causative, _parh-aa-naa_.

The First causative suffix -_aa_ is randomly transcribed as -_a_, -_e_, and -_aa_--often on the same page, [as on p. 32, examples (54), (55)b, (52)b, respectively]; equally randomly, the hyphen notation is used to demarcate this suffix in some instances [as in (52)], but not in others [as in (53)-(55)]. Could these inconsistencies be responsible for Shibatani's assertion that First causatives are lexical?

Through the monograph are scattered judgments which this speaker would question, e.g. (p. 31) "_uth-vaa-naa_ roughly means 'make someone raise something' rather than

'make   someone/something   rise'";   and   (p.   31)   "the   form
rok-naa   'stop   something/someone   corresponds   both   to   the
English   verb   stop   something/someone   and   the   grammatical   form
cause   someone/something   to   stop".

5.2 Previous Studies

The   question   of whether Hindi   causatives   behave   like
simplexes   or   complexes   had   been   investigated,   before
Shibatani   in   Balachandran   1973   (originally 1970),   Kachru
1971,   Kleiman 1971.   These   studies   had   attempted to   resolve
the question by examining causative behavior with respect to
adverbials,   possessive reflexives,   negatives   etc.--some   of
the   very tests that Shibatani was   later to apply to English
and Japanese.   Shibatani was aware   of these earlier   studies
(they   are cited in his bibliography),   but he does not refer
to them in the   text,   or use their findings,   even   though   he
investigates the identical question for Hindi.

Balachandran (1973,   and its earlier 1970 version)   had
argued   that   given   adverbials,   reflexives,   and negatives,
Hindi causatives behave   like   simplexes.   However,   Kachru
(1971)   and Kleiman (1971) presented additional data to show
that this is not always true;   and that word   order,   speaker
variation   (Kachru   1971:78),   and "speakers' presuppositions
about   the   real   world"   (Kleiman   1971:117)   were   often
crucially   determining factors.   Thus,   these earlier studies

had shown that expected tests such as adverbials and reflexives could not be relied upon to yield a systematic distinction between simplex vs. complex in causatives.

One wonders then why Shibatani ignored the findings already available for his question in Hindi--specially since the earlier studies were more complete (because they also considered reflexive and negative tests).

To conclude, the notion of a lexical vs. productive distinction in causatives which links the morphological claims of idiosyncrasy and restriction vs. regularity and productivity with the syntactic claims of simplexes vs. complexes are neither necessary nor desirable in the description of causatives.

References

Aissen, Judith L. 1974. A Syntax of Causative Constructions. Cambridge, Massachusetts: Harvard University dissertation.

Bach, Emmon, and Robert Harms, eds. 1968. Universals in Linguistic Theory. New York: Holt.

Bahl, K. 1967. The Causal Verbs in Hindi. In Language and Areas: Studies Presented to George Bobrinskoy, 6-27. Chicago: University of Chicago, Division of Humanities.

Balachandran, Lakshmi Bai. 1973. A Case Grammar of Hindi. Decennary Publication Series No 7. Agra: Central Institute of Hindi.

Cardona, George. 1978. The Relationships between Causatives and Passives in Indo-Iranian. Collitz Lecture, LSA Summer Meeting.

Chomsky, N. 1957. Syntactic Structures. The Hague: Mouton.

_____. 1965. Aspects of the Theory of Syntax. Cambridge, Massachusetts: MIT Press.

_____. 1970. Remarks on Nominalization. In R. Jacobs and P. Rosenbaum 1970:184-221.

Chomsky, N., and M. Halle. 1968. The Sound Patterns of English. New York: Harper and Row.

Cole, Peter. 1976. The Grammatical Role of the Causee in Universal Grammar. University of Illinois, unpublished MS.

Cole, Peter, and Jerrold M. Sadock, eds. 1977. Syntax and Semantics. Vol. 8: Grammatical Relations. New York: Academic Press.

Comrie, Bernard. 1976a. The Syntax of Causative Constructions: Cross-Linguistic Similarities and Divergences. In Shibatani 1976:261-312.

------. 1976b. Review article: Xolodovič, ed., Tipologija kauzatvnyx konstrukcij. Language 52.2:479-488.

Fillmore, Charles. 1968. The Case for Case. In Bach and Harms 1968:1-90.

------. 1971. Some Problems for Case Grammar. Working Papers in Linguistics 10:245-265. Columbus: Ohio State University.

------. 1977. The Case for Case Reopened. In Cole and Sadock 1977:59-81.

Fodor, J. A. 1970. Three Reasons for Not Deriving 'Kill' from 'Cause to Die'. Linguistic Inquiry 1.4:429-438.

Givon, Talmy. 1976. Some Constraints on Bantu Causativization. In Shibatani 1976:325-351.

Grahame-Bailey, T. 1950. Teach Yourself Hindustani. London: English University Press.

Greenberg, J. H. 1963. Some Universals of Grammar with Particular Reference to the Order of Meaningful Elements. In J. H. Greenberg, ed., Universals of Language, 73-113. Cambridge, Massachusetts: MIT Press.

Gumperz, John J., with A. B. Singh and C. M. Naim. 1967. Conversational Hindi-Urdu. Vols. 1 and 2, Devanagari ed. Delhi: Radhakrishna Prakashan.

Jackendoff, R. 1975. Morphological and Semantic Regularities in the Lexicon. Language 51:639-671.

Jacobs, Roderick A., and Peter S. Rosenbaum, eds. 1970. Readings in English Transformational Grammar. Waltham, Massachusetts: Ginn.

Jain, Jagdish. 1977. The Passive in Universal Grammar. San Francisco State University MS.

Kachru, Yamuna. 1966. An Introduction to Hindi Syntax. Urbana: Department of Linguistics, University of Illinois.

_____. 1971. Causative Sentences in Hindi Revisited. In Papers on Hindi Syntax I.2:75-103. Urbana: Department of Linguistics, University of Illinois.

------. 1976. On the Semantics of the Causative Construction in Hindi-Urdu. In Shibatani 1976:353-369.

Katz, J., and P. Postal. 1964. An Integrated Theory of Linguistic Descriptions. Cambridge, Massachusetts:

MIT Press.

Kellogg, S. H. 1972. A Grammar of the Hindi Language. New Delhi: Oriental Books Reprint Corporation. (This appears to be a reprint of the 1938 third edition, which was only slightly revised from the 1893 second edition.)

Kleiman, Angela B. 1971. Some Aspects of the Causative Construction in Hindi. In Papers in Hindi Syntax 1.2:104-135. Urbana: Department of Linguistics, University of Illinois.

Krishnamurti, Bh. 1971. Causative Constructions in Indian Languages: Some Semantic and Syntactic Aspects. Indian Linguistics 32.1.18-35.

Lakoff, G. 1970. Irregularity in Syntax. New York: Holt.

McCawley, J. 1968. Lexical Insertion in a Transformational Grammar without Deep Structure. In Papers from the Fourth Regional Meeting, Chicago Linguistic Society, 71-80.

McGregor, R. S. 1972. Outline of Hindi Grammar. Oxford: Clarendon Press. Masica, Colin. 1976. A Study of the Distribution of Certain Syntactic and semantic Features in Relation to the definability of an Indian Linguistic Area. Chicago: University of Chicago Press.

Partee, B. 1971. On the Requirement that Transformations Preserve Meaning. In C. Fillmore and T. Langendoen, ed., Studies in Linguistic Semantics. New York: Holt.

Pray, Bruce R.   1970.   Topics in Hindi-Urdu Grammar. Research Monograph No. 1. Berkeley: Center for South and Southeast Asian Studies, University of California.

Saksena, A. 1970. Vowel Length in Hindi. Unpublished UCLA MS.

------. 1975a.   Review of Balachandran 1973.   Language 51:753-760.

------. 1975b. A Surface Structure Constraint in Hindi. Paper presented at the LSA Annual Meeting.

------. 1978.   A Reanalysis of the Passive in Hindi. Lingua 46:339-353.

------.   1979.   The   Grammar   of   Hindi   Causatives. Unpublished UCLA dissertation.

------.   1980.   Surface Structure Sufficiency and   the Problems for Deep Analyses: Case Marking in Hindi. UCLA MS.

Schachter, Paul M. 1975. A Non Transformational Account of Serial Verbs. Papers from the Fifth Conference on African Linguistics.   Studies in African Languages suppl. 5:253-270.

------. 1976. A Non Transformational Account of Gerundive Nominals in English. Linguistic Inquiry 7.2:205-241.

Sharma, Aryendra. 1972. A Basic Grammar of Modern Hindi. Delhi: Ministry of Education and Social Welfare, Government of India.

Shibatani, M. 1975. A Linguistic Study of Causative Constructions. University of California dissertation, reproduced by Indiana University Linguistics Club, Bloomington, Indiana.

------, ed. 1976. Syntax and Semantics, Vol. 6: The Grammar of Causative Constructions. New York: Academic Press.

Xolodovič, A. A. (ed.). 1969. Tipologija kauzativnyx konstrukcij: morfologiceskij kauzativ. Leningrad, Izdatel'stvo "Nauka".

Zide, A. R. K. 1972. Transitive and Causative in Gorum. Journal of Linguistics 8.2:201-217.